Off with My Head

ALSO BY STASSI SCHROEDER

Next Level Basic

Off with My Head

THE DEFINITIVE BASIC B*TCH HANDBOOK
TO SURVIVING ROCK BOTTOM

STASSI SCHROEDER

G

Gallery Books

NEW YORK LONDON TORONTO SYDNEY NEW DELHI

G

Gallery Books
An Imprint of Simon & Schuster, Inc.
1230 Avenue of the Americas
New York, NY 10020

First Gallery Books hardcover edition April 2022

GALLERY BOOKS and colophon are registered trademarks of Simon & Schuster, Inc.

For information about special discounts for bulk purchases, please contact Simon & Schuster Special Sales at 1-866-506-1949 or business@simonandschuster.com.

The Simon & Schuster Speakers Bureau can bring authors to your live event. For more information or to book an event, contact the Simon & Schuster Speakers Bureau at 1-866-248-3049 or visit our website at www.simonspeakers.com.

Interior design by Jaime Putorti
Illustrations by Hannah M. Brown

Manufactured in the United States of America

10 9 8 7 6 5 4 3 2 1

Library of Congress Cataloging-in-Publication Data
Names: Schroeder, Stassi, author.
Title: Off with my head : the definitive basic bitch handbook to surviving rock bottom / Stassi Schroeder.
Identifiers: LCCN 2021035010 (print) | LCCN 2021035011 (ebook) | ISBN 9781982142551 (hardcover) | ISBN 9781982142568 (paperback) | ISBN 9781982142575 (ebook)
Subjects: LCSH: Schroeder, Stassi. | Women television personalities—United States—Biography. | Vanderpump rules (Television program) | Reality television programs—United States. | Self-realization—Humor.
Classification: LCC PN1992.4.S295 A3 2022 (print) | LCC PN1992.4.S295 (ebook) | DDC 791.4502/8092 [B]—dc23
LC record available at https://lccn.loc.gov/2021035010
LC ebook record available at https://lccn.loc.gov/2021035011

ISBN 978-1-9821-4255-1
ISBN 978-1-9821-4257-5 (ebook)

For Hattford,

you saved me.

Contents

CONTENTS

Off with My Head

Welcome to the Guillotine

The only way I can accurately describe the year 2020 is that, for the most part, it felt just like the final season of *Game of Thrones*. Yes, I'm still talking about *GOT* long after the show ended and everyone has now moved on to *Bridgerton* or *Emily in Paris* or whatever. I've seen all those tweets telling me to get a new television show shtick, but I am still not over the final season of *Game of Thrones*, and I may never be. Just let it be, people. Let me live out loud, even if I'm talking about this show for the next forty years.

Before it all went to hell, the year 2020 was going to be the best year of my life. I was going on my second national podcast tour, where I wore bedazzled tuxedo jackets and met amazing fans across the country. I was finishing my second book, which was going to be full of career and life advice about living your most badass basic bitch life. I was still on *Vanderpump Rules*, and we had big things planned for the show, but we all know how that turned out. I was also planning a fall 2020 wedding, but we all know how 2020 weddings turned out. Shout out to all my Covid brides. I see you, bitches.

To top it all off, I had also just sold the rights to *Next Level Basic* to turn it into an animated series (so major!). Besides getting engaged and being on top of the world career-wise, I bought a house for the first time, and I was busy morphing into a Bridezilla and planning my dream Italian wedding. 2020 showed so much freaking promise—so I probably should've known better. I should have read the signs. That shit was way too good to be true. With *GOT*, the final season was supposed to be the best season, right? Daenerys was supposed to marry Jon Snow, and they were supposed to have a little baby Khaleesi who would be the future ruler of pretty much everything. But that's not what happened. AT ALL.

Instead, we were delivered the actual worst season of television in history, so much so that I have never seen our country more united and bonded in anything than we were with our collective distaste for the final season of *Game of Thrones*. Until I saw us all bonded in our stress over Covid. SPOILER ALERT: Daenerys did not give birth to a cute baby queen, and she did not marry Jon Snow. No, she burned down a city and got stabbed by her boo. BUZZ. KILL. And as if it couldn't have gotten any worse, Bran ends up winning *GOT* and becoming the ruler? *Bran?* Bran, the little weasel who was the literal cause of every bad thing that ever happened? He became the three-eyed raven and has psychic visions, and he doesn't use that gift to help his friends or family? What is your deal? I can't. I. JUST. CAN'T. And that is exactly how I feel about 2020. There would be no magical Roman wedding for us in 2020. My tour was postponed one month in. Seriously, I was in Bensalem, Pennsylvania, about to go to my meet and greet before the show. I was putting on my glitter eyeshadow, and I was actually mid sparkle stroke when I received a call that the tour was canceled and I was to be flown home because of Covid.

I packed up my glitter and got on a plane two hours later, and that was the end of my national tour. Forever. My semi-not-quite Beyoncé moment was *dunzo*. That was tough to take, but little did I know that I was about to be a whole lot more dunzo in a mere three months. Like the most dunzo you could actually ever get besides passing away. CANCELED AF. Squared. Times a million. And squared again. I'm not saying I deserve sympathy or pity. I know I brought a lot of this on myself. I am just here to give the facts and share my math skills.

Yep, as you probably know since you're reading this book, I was canceled in 2020 . . . again. I do fully understand my part in all of this, and I am truly, deeply sorry. I also know that for some, "sorry" is just a word, and that I am not owed forgiveness by anyone. I realize that I hurt people like Faith, who you will hear more about, and though I've grown and learned from my mistakes, I realize there may not be forgiveness out there, and that's your prerogative. I can only tell my story, as honestly as I can. Ironic tidbit? A week before I got canceled, I was recording an episode for Katie Maloney's podcast *You're Gonna Love Me*, and she asked me about the first time I got canceled, for remarks and photos I shared that, looking back, were insensitive and wrong. I wrote about this in *Next Level Basic*, but several years ago I posted a photo on Instagram with the caption "Nazi chic" (my initials are SS, and those initials were on my outfit, and well, I added an offensive hashtag as a poor attempt at a joke). I also made comments about the #MeToo movement that I quickly regretted, and learned from. Then there was an Oscars podcast where I said that "all lives matter." All are examples of extreme ignorance. I was living a life of privilege where I never even thought about how jokes or comments like that would affect other people. I felt and still feel so strongly about how wrong I was, and clearly I still had a lot to learn. Kind of like Marie Antoinette, only instead of getting the chance to learn from her mistakes and step back and recognize her privilege, she had her beautifully coiffed head chopped off. (For this reason, I'll be referencing her a lot in this book.)

On Katie's podcast I remember telling her, "You know, I'm sure at some point I'll be canceled again, and the next time I'll know exactly how to deal with it." Yes, I got canceled again, but no, turns out I still didn't know how to deal with it. Being canceled once didn't help or prepare me for this next one. The big one. The *Avengers: Endgame* of all cancels. (Beau would be so proud of me for that reference.) This cancellation was so big, it was like taking home the Emmy, the Golden Globe, the Oscar, *and* the Tony Award in one year, except, you know, the opposite. So yeah, you could say my 2020 was most definitely as horrible as the *GOT* final season.

Despite all that, there was one little sprinkle of joy among the horror. Okay, a big-ass sprinkle of joy: My pregnancy. I have hoped and prayed to be a mom my whole life, so getting pregnant was hands down the best thing that had ever happened to me. If we're going to make sense of this for the sake of my *GOT* metaphor, I'd say this is like the moment Arya kills the Night King. Yes, I just compared the joy of discovering my pregnancy to the joy I felt when a *Game of Thrones* monster was killed. Let's just roll with it. It's a very trippy thing to go through the best thing that ever happened to you and the worst thing that ever happened to you at the same time. I feel like my pregnancy happened at the exact time it was supposed to, because my daughter was the main thing that got me through the hell that was watching my career and everything I had worked for implode. I'm not saying that my 2020 was worse than anyone else's, because we collectively endured one of the toughest years of our lives. Parents had to juggle homeschooling and work, people lost jobs and homes and, most tragic of all, loved ones. There was so much grief and pain all over the world, so I understand I am a tiny drop of it. But still. It sucked.

I mean, like many of you, I truly was living my best life before Covid. I would've toured 365 days a year for the rest of my life if I was allowed to keep going (well, unless I got pregnant). I felt like Lady Gaga. I had my own tour bus, where I got to travel to all these different cities with my fiancé, Beau, and my best friend Taylor Strecker. I got to check into amazing hotels, get my hair done, meet so many of my Khaleesis (aka my podcast listeners) and be onstage in sparkly clothes, with an Aperol spritz in one hand and an engagement ring on the other. Life could not have gotten any better. I will cherish those times FOR-FREAKING-EVER. I just hope I get to do it again one day, and maybe baby Hartford can make some cameo appearances onstage.

The whole "be careful what you wish for" thing is real. In early 2020 I didn't have a single day off, and I would complain about wanting to just sit on my couch and watch TV and have a break, even though I loved what I was doing. But it's like that horror movie *Fantasy Island* (not the 1970s show), where they think all their fantasies are going to come true but then those fantasies go horribly wrong. My fantasy went horribly wrong. Instead of that one day on the couch I longed for, I got every single day of the year on the couch, on a loop, with nowhere to go because the country had shut down and there were paparazzi stalking my house. It was even scary ordering Postmates!

Like I said, most of us experienced some sort of rock bottom in 2020, whether it was losing loved ones or jobs, anxiety about the pandemic, dealing with kids being home all day, or canceling all your awesome trips and plans and weddings. I realize that there are varying degrees of rock bottom. I know that my situation could be so much worse, and that my rock bottom is not the same as someone else's rock bottom. If you've listened to my podcast over the years, you'll know that I've used this term to describe any time I've felt like I was in a seriously low place. I want to make it very clear that the way I'm referring to rock bottom in this book is to reference a generally shitty situation, and not to measure or diminish anyone's personal experience. Listen, there's a part of me that wants a little sympathy after a hard year, even though I know I was part of the problem. But I'm mainly writing this book because I've missed you, and I feel like I have some things to say about pulling yourself out of rock bottom and learning from your mistakes, and

I hope you'll go along for the ride. I may not know a lot, but I do feel like I'm somewhat of an authority on making mistakes, getting knocked down, trying to learn from what went wrong, and moving forward. I've been at rock bottom quite a few times, in ways that were so public and felt so final. Hopefully my stories can help someone else find their way out of their own worst times. Or maybe you'll just read this book and then tweet about how much you hate me. And you know what—go ahead! I've heard it all before. I'm good.

In case some of you are worried that I have gone soft, I am still a proud basic bitch. I'm now just a basic bitch with a tiny basic bitch sidekick. I'm a mom who is a little more layered and who is trying to be better. I have more on my plate nowadays. My life isn't simply fanciful and easy. I have a mortgage instead of rent. I have another human being to think about, and with that comes the responsibility to be the best version of myself. I need to be the best role model I can be for my daughter. Being a basic bitch is about embracing what you like regardless of what it looks like. My basic bitch tendencies just look a little different now. I think I'm learning that it's not enough to *just* be a basic bitch. I want to be a basic bitch who lives in a way that contributes to the world in a positive way. I still love trash TV and monogrammed everything. During pregnancy I missed wine nights dearly. I still love pumpkin spice lattes in October, but I'm also very much into doing the work to better myself while I drink my latte or dip my pizza in Ranch. I guess you could say I'm a little more well-rounded? Being held accountable in such a public way changed me. Being pregnant changed me. Becoming a mom changed me. Life is still fun AF, but it's a little more serious now, and trying to crawl out of what has felt like rock bottom has a way of putting life in perspective, and sometimes changing you for the better.

I also just miss the hell out of my Khaleesis. Hopefully by writing this book I can shed some light on what happened with me, have some fun, and put some good into the world. I'd love to prove that those Khaleesis weren't wrong for giving me second (or third) chances. Some of this was written while I was heavily preggo, and some of it while I had a newborn who did mom-and-baby OOTDs with me. So, it has been, and still is, a journey.

All I can say is, I'm trying, and I hope these stories will make you laugh, make you feel understood, or just entertain you for a while. I did a lot of work on myself, looking at the ways I'd gone wrong in the past so I wouldn't ever make the same mistakes again. I did a lot of that internal work while pregnant, without a single glass of pinot grigio or an Aperol spritz! I did it while waddling around, sober, wondering why my feet were getting so swollen and terrified I'd never fit into my cute shoes again. At least I didn't suffer Marie Antoinette's fate, because girlfriend supposedly lost one of her cute heels on the way to the guillotine to get beheaded. I just couldn't fit into mine because I was pregnant, so I guess I should consider myself lucky. One thing I've learned, though, is that there are more important things in life than cute heels. Not many, but a few . . .

So, cheers to crawling out of rock bottom, together.

Stassi

CHAPTER 1

The Canceling

*The one thing I would ask when you pick up this book, is that you read this chapter in its entirety before you make any judgments. It reads in chronological order. This is complex and no line or paragraph could stand on its own.

First things first: I know I made mistakes. Huge ones. I know I'm the only one to blame, and I've been trying hard to do better. Still, I'd be lying if I said the Canceling of 2020 didn't feel like a straight-up horror movie, only a horror movie that is not at all fun to watch. At least, not for me. And I freaking love horror movies.

Just imagine making a terrible mistake, but one that has nothing to do with how good you are at your job, and one that doesn't truly reflect who you are. You're fired because of that mistake, and no one else will hire you because they don't want to be seen with you. You're told to stay quiet. You're already ashamed of the mistake you made. You already want to fix it. But on top of that, every single person you know or have ever met knows about this mistake. Strangers know about your shameful mistake. Your UPS guy knows about it, the grocery store clerk knows, the bartender at your happy hour spot, your children's school knows it, your doctors and your exes and your neighbors know.

Half of them are supportive and call to offer condolences or support. The other half write all over your Facebook page or your Instagram account condemning you for your mistakes. They use horrible language, telling you you're done, you'll never work again, you're trash, you don't deserve another chance. They write that you should probably kill yourself. Those people even go on your friends' and family members' personal social media accounts and harass them and tell them they're horrible people who won't work again unless they denounce or disown you. Imagine they tell your husband/wife that he/she won't work again unless your significant other divorces you. They say your unborn child is a racist. It all makes you want to hide in a dark closet and never come out. That's exactly what being canceled feels like. But worse. Marie Antoinette was once the most hated woman in France, and for a while, I was the most hated person on the internet, which is not nearly as glamorous.

Maybe you're wondering what I did to get canceled? If you're reading this book, you probably know, but if you're not aware and you just found this book on the sidewalk or something, here it is: Faith Stowers was a cast member on *Vanderpump Rules* for a season, and during that time she slept with Jax when he was dating Brittany, who was and is one of my closest friends. During the season, Kristen Doute, my fellow cast member, started getting texts from people alleging that Faith had stolen from them in the past and saying that Faith was in a surveillance video showing someone stealing. Then we saw a news article with the video still of the woman who was accused of stealing, so we called the tip line. We (stupidly) thought it might be Faith, partly because multiple people had been texting Kristen saying it was her, and also in our very flawed detective work, we thought the description of the woman's tattoos sounded like Faith's. Kristen left a message on the tip line and gave her own contact information, and we never heard back, so that was the end of it. To my knowledge, Faith never even knew about the call until she heard me talk about it on a podcast about a year later. I wasn't hiding it, but I also shouldn't have been talking and joking about it. We also shouldn't have made that phone call, but I didn't understand that at the time.

When the incident was brought up again years later, so many variables of the story became twisted by the media, which became incredibly frustrating. Once the online gossip machine starts grinding away, it's almost impossible to stop it. I read articles that said we were playing a prank on Faith by calling the cops. That was the most infuriating lie—that it was a prank—but at the time I didn't feel I had the right to defend myself. It took me a while to process my feelings and recognize how layered it all was. It took time to recognize that Faith felt it was about race because there *is* an actual serious problem between the Black community and the police in America. I understand that now, but I didn't then. I had a lot to learn.

The Canceling didn't actually happen overnight, like one of the *Purge* movies. It happened over the course of seven days, kind of like the biblical creation of Earth, but this was all about destruction, and there was no fun day of rest. Each day brought a new blow. It started with my sponsors, which were calls that I had completely expected, understood, and prepared for. I didn't get angry when brands decided to distance themselves from me. We're all out here just trying to survive and protect the things we built, so if a sponsor *quietly* parts ways with me, they have my respect. However, I do get angry when sponsors use my scandal as an opportunity to highlight themselves while dragging me through the mud. You know, those brands that tweet out 3,847,623 times how I'm despicable while literally @ing me and hashtagging the situation so they get all the trolls as followers. Yeah, that angers me.

IN THE BEGINNING THERE WAS A CANCELING

1 LOST SPONSORS.

2 LOST MORE SPONSORS. (THERE WAS NO) REJOICING)

3 PR AGENT LEFT

4 LOST TALENT AGENTS

5 FIRED FROM VANDERPUMP

6 LOST PODCAST

7 LOST ANIMATED SERIES

AND THEN SOMEONE RESTED BUT IT WASN'T STASSI...

Losing my sponsors hurt, but it didn't break my spirit. I've been through this before, unfortunately. What really shook my world was being so publicly fired from my PR company. I had been with my publicist for almost seven years. She had become one of my closest friends. I spent more time with her than I did most of my best friends. We traveled together, told each other everything, and she was one of the first people to know about my pregnancy. I loved her. When she called to tell me the news, it was two hours after I had posted my apology on Instagram. An apology that not only had to get approved by Bravo (ironic considering they fired me two days later) but also an apology that those very publicists had helped me write. Yes, I had help with the apology that was not so well received. Maybe it was too little, too late for people, or maybe nothing I could have said at that time would have made a difference. I want to be transparent, so I admit that I was not ready to apologize at that time. I hadn't yet fully grasped why this was about race. I was scared, and I was being pressured from anyone and everyone to put one out. Looking back, I wish I had never issued it and that I had written my own, on my own time. All my instincts were telling me to hold off. I needed time to process what was happening and process my feelings, and not just pretend I was innocent. When your life is so public, there isn't much time for contemplation. People want answers and apologies, and then they want to rip you apart for those answers and apologies. It's not like I could go to a Buddhist retreat for a month and then come back and address the issues. I had people on Instagram screaming at me!

I needed time to learn where my mistakes were coming from and why they were so wrong. I needed time to truly understand it in a meaningful way, instead of pretending to grasp the full scope right away. But I caved to all the pressure and I wrote an apology, and then I let my publicist rewrite the apology I had already written. I let her boss have approval, and I let Bravo have approval. All of that approval took days. And people were tweeting and commenting, asking where the apology was. Well, I had written an apology, but a million other people who were supposed to be on my side were rewriting and approving it and taking their time, only to fire me hours after it was released.

I will never forget the call. My publicist was crying. I was so confused and kept asking her what happened. She said her boss (the owner of the PR firm) was terminating our contract. I mean, *I* paid *them*, but they could still fire me for the exact scandals that they were not only aware of for years, but that they helped me through? They didn't think they were fire-worthy before, but in June 2020 they sure did. What especially hurt in this situation was that I wouldn't get to work with my personal publicist again. The woman who I spent so much time with, who I would trust my life with. She wasn't just my publicist, she was my manager and my friend. We both sat there crying on the phone, and I assured her it was all going to be okay. We could still be friends after all, right? She sobbed through the conversation and said of course. I never heard from her again.

I don't know if her boss was threatening her and maybe she wasn't allowed to contact me. Regardless, it hurt. That PR firm didn't just quietly part ways. They publicized it—the exact opposite of what a publicist's job is, which is to protect your reputation. Your PR is supposed to be the last one standing with you. And that is what started the chain reaction that made this the mother of all cancels.

When my PR told the press they were dropping me, *Variety*, which is a very reputable news site, picked it up and decided to write a piece on it. A publicist dropping a client and publicizing it is kind of a big deal. *Variety* then reached out to my agency to ask where they stood. My agency had to make a decision that day, since the article was going to be released that evening. My agents were another group of people who had become my friends. I loved my agents, still do. It was like a big family. I had been so proud that I had surrounded myself with a team I liked so much. We all had the same goals and focus, we all got on great; it had been perfect. Until it wasn't. Again, I am not saying I'm blameless here. I'm just telling you about my seven days of destruction as I remember them.

The day after my PR dropped me is when I got the call from my agent. She was also in tears, and she said they had been fighting with the board of the agency all day to keep me but that the higher-ups wouldn't allow it. An article in *Variety* was the last straw, I guess. Just like that, my team was wiped out. My PR, my manager, my main agent, my book agent, my sponsor agent, my podcast agent, my touring agent. I didn't know who I was even allowed to email or contact in order to get copies of my contracts and important information. I was lost. I was also very newly (and secretly) pregnant, with people telling me to stay calm, which wasn't always easy.

I woke up on the fifth morning to texts from Kristen Doute.

She was absolutely hysterical, and there were missed calls from my lawyer and from my *Vanderpump Rules* producers. I immediately knew without being told. Bravo had made an announcement that the two of us would not return to *Vanderpump Rules*. I cried with Kristen. I cried with my producers, who also cried with me. Most of my producers actually found out about the firings on social media. They were outraged. They had known all about what happened with Faith—they'd been around when the original call to the tip line happened. They had pleaded with Bravo and said that our behavior was encouraged by being on *Vanderpump Rules*. I mean, this is the shit *Vanderpump Rules* is about: exposing people, calling them out. I'm not trying to justify what I did whatsoever, but looking back I was motivated by the fact that Faith had played a dirty role on our show that year by hooking up with Jax behind Brittany's back and blackmailing him with audio. Our producers begged for our jobs, but it was hopeless.

I got one call from Lisa Vanderpump two hours after I got the news, but I was in the fetal position crying, so, yeah, I wasn't really calling people back. A long time after that she texted me, and I ended up running into her a year later, at the Polo Lounge in Beverly Hills. Beau and I were with our friends Taylor Strecker and Taylor Donohue, and thankfully I was three martinis in. I'd been so nervous to run into Lisa because of everything that had happened, but our conversation was oddly comforting. It was nice to see her and have things on good terms. I have no idea where our relationship will go, but I wish her the best.

Kristen came over to my house that morning, and it was the

first time I had seen her since our very public and very dramatic falling-out (more on that later). We sat in my house all day as paparazzi started to line up outside. My assistant, Lo French, went to Target to buy curtains to cover my windows so they couldn't see in (I didn't go with her because I would have been stalked). I felt like a pregnant prisoner in my own home. Beau encouraged me to hide downstairs in the bedroom since it was one of the only rooms people couldn't see into. I did, only to come out for food and water, like a mole. I didn't feel safe even in my own house. But it wasn't over yet. Every time I felt like I had nothing left, no energy or tears, there was always a new day and one more thing that imploded. On day six, my podcast company dropped me and erased every episode of *Straight Up with Stassi* from iTunes, as if it never existed. Almost six years of podcasting, vanished.

The next day, all the venues that were scheduled for my tour started canceling, and my animated series deal with Sony was terminated. I was so canceled, I thought my gynecologist was going to drop me. I'm not even joking.

A few days later, Beau woke me up at 7:00 a.m. and said my new crisis publicist, Steve, had been calling nonstop. Yes, I hired a crisis publicist, *because he was one of the only publicists who would go near me.* I groggily called Steve back, and he told me someone had leaked my pregnancy to *Us Weekly*. That was when I just finally, completely lost it. I was hurt beyond repair. I had made it through a week of firings and people slaughtering my name, but now this was taken from me? The one thing in my life that was mine, that I thought no one could ever take from me. Who would do such a thing? Who would call *Us* freaking *Weekly*, and spill a secret that was so deeply personal?

I won't say the name, but I have a hunch who it was. I'm not angry anymore, because I don't have space for that in my life. It would be nice if the karma gods came and bit them on the ass though.

I wasn't even through my first trimester. I was only ten weeks along when the pregnancy was leaked. I had successfully evaded the paparazzi by scheduling my gynecologist appointments at the crack of dawn, before photographers arrived at my house for the day. After I was canceled, I had decided I wanted to "Kylie Jenner" my pregnancy, meaning I wanted to hole up at home as if I were a glamorous recluse living in a compound—but *not* like a mole. I always thought it was such a boss move of Kylie's. Since my career had imploded, I wanted to be pregnant quietly and privately. I felt torn apart by everyone, so why would I then share this most special thing with those very people? I also knew that people just didn't want to hear from me. It wasn't my time to be out there hashtagging #blessed and #pregnant (not that I would do that, but still). It was my time to take a step back and be respectful. But *someone* in my life decided to take my baby and spin it.

Like I said, I'm 98 percent certain I know who spawned #baby-gate. Journalists wouldn't tell me who leaked it, but there are only a few people in my life who I know talk to the press. Whoever it was, it was truly unforgivable (unless of course they realized the error of their ways and owned up to it and sincerely apologized— I'm waiting!). My pregnancy became something that some people thought I was spinning for attention, and I couldn't do anything about it. Defending myself would only make them attack more. I had people commenting that my unborn baby was racist. I couldn't leave my house because of the paparazzi outside, and when I did leave the house, they would take a photo, and people would think I was unremorseful and staging photo ops.

I so desperately wanted to scream from the rooftops (or Instagram) that there were photographers everywhere and I wasn't staging anything, but no one wanted to hear from me at this point, and I get that. I swallowed every comment or assumption people made about what my life was like and what I was doing. I left town to go to Utah with Beau, Katie, and Tom Schwartz, and an asshole paparazzi followed my car all the way to Las Vegas. I'm assuming he thought he was going to get some killer photo of a recently fired, newly pregnant, drunk, racist, unremorseful Stassi arriving at Caesars Palace without a mask during a pandemic. He must have been pissed when he drove back to LA without a scandal to sell.

So that was my seven days in hell, in a nutshell. Did I do things to get myself in that position? Yes. Did I realize that I had a lot of listening and learning to do? For sure. And I'm still learning and growing.

When everything started to snowball, I felt like I didn't deserve forgiveness. It was like the whole world didn't want me to learn or be better. They just wanted me gone. I made a mistake, and I was erased for it. I couldn't even defend myself, because so many people didn't want to hear it. I wasn't allowed. Cancel culture is medieval. It's counterproductive. I think people sometimes confuse cancel culture with whatever social movement is happening during a certain time. Social movements and cancel culture are two separate things. I deserved to be called out. I wish I would have been *called in*, to be held accountable and to have a discussion. I want to be part of the discussion, I want to be corrected. But to take away the ability to support myself is another level. That's some Roman gladiator fight-to-the-death type shit. Don't even get me started on the people who insulted my unborn baby.

Eventually, I had to turn my shame to guilt. Instead of feeling like I was a bad person, I came to see that what I did was bad, and I could work to change. In cancel culture, you're either good or you're bad, since there is nothing in between. Call me out and challenge me and correct me instead of deleting me. Deleting me leaves me no room to grow or change. It makes it impossible for me to ask the questions and be part of the dialogue that helps with educating. With cancel culture, there is no space to figure things out and make mistakes. It just doesn't make sense to me. Instead of canceling people, wouldn't you want to encourage them to educate themselves knowing they could become a real ally for your cause?

I think one of the most profound things I've learned is that just because it wasn't about race for me doesn't mean that it wasn't about race for Faith. I understand that there is unconscious bias, but I really was defending my friend Brittany, who was hurt by Faith. I spent a while being angry about what happened. But the more I learned, the more I realized that with every situation, each of us is bringing our own worldviews and history into that very situation. Faith brought her experience as a Black woman, and I brought mine as a white woman—a white woman who has never had to think twice about the police or what that means for other people, which is basically a pillar of white privilege. So while Kristen and I didn't feel this situation was about race, it was for Faith, and because of that, it *was* about race.

Kristen and I messed up because we obviously weren't 100 percent sure the woman in the photo was Faith. I know I was in the wrong because I acted on gossip instead of facts. I didn't witness Faith stealing anything, so I had zero right to accuse her. I should never have been discussing this on a podcast or in public, especially in such a braggy and flippant way. I sensationalized it for the sake of a good podcast story, and I regret that immensely.

I handled all of it incorrectly. I was wrong. I just need people to understand this wasn't motivated by her race. Was I driven by nefarious motives? Absolutely. I can't deny that. She had deeply hurt my friend. I was absolutely motivated by that, and I was motivated by the fact that I thought she was guilty of these crimes. I basically thought I was the karma god, just dishing it out exactly where I felt it should be.

It took a good few weeks for me to realize that hiring a diversity coach was a route I wanted to take, because the first few weeks after the Canceling, I was still angry and confused. But eventually, because the George Floyd protests and the worldwide civil rights movement that followed were so powerful, I knew I wanted to learn more. Even though all the trolls and cancelers out there didn't want me to be better or become part of the solution, I knew I wanted to be better. It took a while to feel like I had the right to even try. I think what really helped push me to seek out a coach is the fact that I had messed up before. The "Nazi chic" photo I posted to Instagram and the podcast I did in 2017 about #OscarsSoWhite made me realize that I had fucked up too many times and I needed to make a bold move to educate myself. Simply watching a TED Talk, or reading an article on racism, or discussing Black Lives Matter with friends wasn't going to suffice.

I needed to put myself in an uncomfortable position to have these discussions, particularly with a stranger who had dedicated their career to deepening people's understanding about race. It took a while to find someone to work with because whoever that person was going to be, they had to sign an NDA (nondisclosure agreement), agreeing to keep our relationship confidential. I needed to be able to speak freely, ask questions freely, accidentally mess up freely—without someone going to the press and repeating everything I said. Surprisingly (or not), most people didn't want to sign the NDA, which I will never understand. What were they planning to do with the details of our classes and conversations? My crisis publicist was able to help me find someone who agreed right away. Thank the lord for May Snowden, the sweetest most nonjudgmental human. I never expected to actually look forward to our Zoom meetings. At first I was so nervous. Talking about race isn't exactly fun. It's uncomfortable, especially when you have to examine your own participation in racial matters. But May made me feel so incredibly comfortable. Even if she was secretly judging me, I never felt it once.

May started each conversation by telling me to be kind to myself. This is how you teach people to be better, not by shutting them down but by giving them a safe space to grow, and a safe space to ask questions. My biggest issue with cancel culture isn't that I was canceled. I don't feel like a victim anymore. That doesn't mean I don't sometimes still feel sad about what happened. My issue is that it shuts down the conversation entirely. It shuts down communication. And nothing gets resolved when you shut down communication. So every Friday at 1:00 p.m., I would Zoom with May. We began by examining what it means to be *culturally competent*, a phrase I personally think is very underused. To be culturally competent means that you're someone who not only understands your own culture but you also have the knowledge and awareness of other cultures, and you know how to communicate and effectively interact with people from other cultures. This is embarrassing, but I always thought of myself as someone who was culturally well-rounded. I mean, my mentality was "I've been to Europe 872,364 times, so of course I know how to interact with other cultures." EYE ROLL. How obnoxious am I? Privileged to the nth degree.

To truly be culturally competent, May explained, you need to constantly be educating yourself about other cultures. There is this American attitude that people from everywhere else need to conform to our customs. Our children aren't taught enough about how to interact with other cultures. Diving into the different aspects of cultural competence made me realize there is so much I don't know. We discussed how emotional intelligence plays a huge role in being culturally competent, and I was delighted to discover that unlike your IQ, you can actually work on and practice having a higher emotional intelligence. Hope is not lost for people like me out there! Anyone who has messed up before can practice being better, if they want to.

After a few weeks with May, I had an aha moment and I recognized an area where I could try to make a difference and not just talk. For those couple of weeks, we focused on Black history. She assigned me documentaries to watch (like Henry Louis Gates Jr.'s *The African Americans: The Many Rivers to Cross*), podcasts to listen to, and books and articles to read (like *So You Want to Talk About Race* by Ijeoma Oluo and "White Privilege: Unpacking the Invisible Knapsack" by Peggy McIntosh). I began to feel so deeply ashamed about the Oscars podcast I did years ago. I wish I could take it back. I cringe and have a visceral reaction every time I think about it. Yes, I had already learned from that mistake, already been canceled for it, already atoned for it, and I even wrote about it in my last chapter of *Next Level Basic*, but this time I felt so much more ashamed. I just understood entirely and completely how wrong I was. I couldn't even believe I had questioned Black Lives Matter. The realization that I was one of those freaking Karens who say "What about all lives matter?" was a seriously tough pill to swallow.

If I had been taught about Black history (and I don't just mean the things we're taught in February for Black History Month), all the details and depth of Black history—about bias, about systemic racism, about how the Black community has been consistently oppressed for four hundred years—maybe I wouldn't have said those things. If I had truly understood, if I had been taught the depth of all of that, I would never have done that podcast. I would never have even had those thoughts. I know why Black

Lives Matter. Because they have been oppressed, they haven't been given a fair chance, and they are being killed. And until Black lives matter, then all lives can't matter. Learning all this while pregnant, and then having a daughter, made me think about what I'll teach her. Children from a young age should be consistently taught not only about Black history but about unconscious bias and systemic racism. I'm not trying to say that I, Stassi, can change racism in America, but I am saying I can try to do my small part in how I raise my child. I hadn't even heard the words *systemic racism* until the Canceling, and I wanted to make sure my daughter grows up aware and conscious of all of this.

I became obsessed with how I was going to teach my daughter how to be someone with as few biases as possible. With May, I discussed and role-played how to handle my unconscious bias when I recognize it in myself. We discussed how to check your privilege and why it's so important. There is so much shame associated with racism that we are terrified to admit any bias. May helped me understand that once you take that shame out of it, it allows you to speak freely and have these conversations, which is the only way to effectively learn.

For so long, I thought the worst thing that ever happened to me was the fact that the public was calling me racist, and I've realized that if *that* is the worst thing that has ever happened to me, well then how privileged am I? I was someone who got so defensive when I was accused of racism. And I now know that being defensive is one of the worst things you can be when it comes to understanding. Again, it shuts down the conversation. All of this was because of my ignorance and privilege.

It was my fault I've been ignorant, and it's my fault that I didn't seek this knowledge earlier. But I'm not ignorant anymore, and I'm actively trying to learn every day. Our country has a very big problem, and I was a part of that problem. But now I want to be a part of the solution. My biggest takeaway to help other people who may be in my position is to explain that we're all going to mess up, we're all going to at some point say something incorrectly that hurts someone else, but you have to keep trying. We need to stop being so afraid of the word *racist*, because that's keeping us from having meaningful conversations. You have to open up the conversations instead of shutting them down, and keep trying. Keep listening, and keep trying.

Rock-Bottom TAKEAWAY

Getting called out wasn't my fave thing to ever happen, but being called out in such a public, shameful way in 2020 actually helped me become a better, more multilayered basic bitch (I hope). No matter how bad it seems in the moment, the worst thing you can do is throw a lifelong pity party and blame others, and the best thing you can do is look at where you went wrong and learn from that. It's not fun. There is nothing glamorous about it. But it does help you crawl out of rock bottom and emerge a better human. Not all cancellations are public. Some are between friends or coworkers or family, but they cut just as deep. So roll up your bedazzled sleeves (or the sleeves of the tattered robe you've been wearing nonstop because you're at rock bottom and totes don't feel like dressing cute), get honest with yourself, and try to do better next time. Oh, and block the haters. They will not bring out your best basic bitch self.

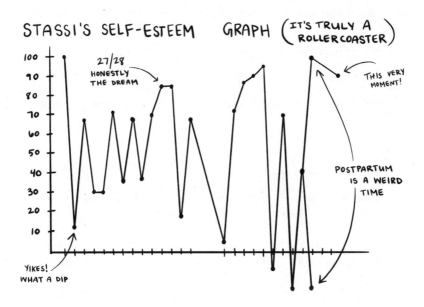

STASSI'S SELF-ESTEEM GRAPH (IT'S TRULY A ROLLER COASTER)

27/28 HONESTLY THE DREAM

THIS VERY MOMENT!

POSTPARTUM IS A WEIRD TIME

YIKES! WHAT A DIP

Stassi's Self-Esteem Graph
(FROM CHILDHOOD UNTIL NOW)

* **100 PERCENT**: Born confident AF. I'm a baby after all; I don't know any better.

✳ **11 PERCENT:** Age six. Boy makes fun of me for having a lot of moles. What a dick.

✳ **67 PERCENT:** Age thirteen. Elected school president. Damn, you guys like me, you really like me. Or you're scared of me. Either way, confidence level rising.

✳ **30 PERCENT:** Age fourteen. Auditioned for *Into the Woods* and got cast as a freaking singing tree. Not ideal.

✳ **30 PERCENT:** Ages fifteen to sixteen. WHY WHY WHY DID I GO SEMI GOTH AND DYE MY HAIR BLACK AND DO *THE AMAZING RACE*? Awkward stage in full effect.

✳ **72 PERCENT:** Age seventeen. Voted "Most Talented" in my senior class. Things are starting to look up again. I feel like a badass.

✳ **35 PERCENT:** Age eighteen. Freshman year of college is cool and all, having an apartment is cool and all, but WHO AM I? WHAT IS MY FUTURE? I'M CONCERNED.

✳ **69 PERCENT:** Age twenty-one. Got a job at SUR because they liked my headshot. Interesting. Should I try modeling? Lol.

✳ **36 PERCENT:** Age twenty-three. Season one of *Vanderpump Rules* airs and *wow* . . . people really hate me.

✳ **70 PERCENT:** Age twenty-four. Season two of *Vanderpump Rules* airs and okay . . . at least people love to hate me.

✳ **85 PERCENT:** Age twenty-seven. My podcast is successful as shit. How did this happen?!

✳ **85 PERCENT:** Age twenty-eight. Maintaining my 85 percent self-esteem level by discovering OOTDs.

✳ **16 PERCENT:** Age twenty-nine. My forty millionth breakup with Patrick.

✳ **68 PERCENT:** (Also) age twenty-nine: I just met Beau. I think he likes me.

✳ **3 PERCENT:** Age twenty-nine. Made horrible "Nazi chic" joke on Instagram. Life over. I fucked up.

✳ **73 PERCENT:** Age thirty. I'm in love with Beau. He's in love with me. Also I just learned how to put false eyelashes on in under three minutes. Things are looking up again.

✳ **86 PERCENT:** Age thirty. *Next Level Basic* is a *New York Times* bestseller! I am feeling GREAT.

✳ **90 PERCENT:** Age thirty-one. I'm engaged! I just bought my very first house—in the Hollywood Hills. I can't believe my luck; this is going to be the best year ever!

✳ **95 PERCENT:** Age thirty-one. I'm on a live podcast tour, and I'm actually selling out big venues. How did I trick all these people into thinking I'm so cool?! Life could not be better!

✳ **–15 PERCENT:** Age thirty-one. I'm quarantined because of coronavirus. I'm falling apart. I feel worthless. I only wear sweatpants. I don't remember what an OOTD is. Why can't I stop eating? Tour is canceled. What is to become of me?!

✳ **70 PERCENT:** Age thirty-one. I'm pregnant, oh my GOSH. Yes, quarantining is awful, but I am PREGNANT. At least now I have an excuse to keep eating.

✳ **–100 PERCENT:** Age thirty-one. Canceled AF—I've lost my job, my agents, my PR, my podcast, etc. The world thinks I'm racist, and I'm scared to go outside.

✳ **40 PERCENT:** Age thirty-two. Still canceled AF but looking on the bright side. This is an opportunity to be better, I still have my loved ones, I'm healthy, and I'm getting ready to have a baby.

✳ Can you be **100 PERCENT AND –100 PERCENT** at the same time?! Because that's exactly how I felt postpartum. I felt like such a proud rock star of a woman after giving birth, but there's nothing like the realness of a swollen yet deflated postpartum body that serves as a milk machine to make you feel insecure.

✳ **90 PERCENT:** Age thirty-three. Second book (THIS BOOK) is out! Life is back to normal(ish). The future is totally unknown, but at least I have my OOTD mirror and my baby girl!

Types of Friends You'll Meet at Rock Bottom

The One You're In It With: It's no secret that Kristen Doute and I weren't exactly on speaking terms when the Canceling began to happen. Our last season of *Vanderpump Rules* focused heavily on the demise of our friendship. So much toxicity had seeped in, and we became incapable of getting along. There were too many fights, too many betrayals, and I made a decision to cut it off. I've always been of the mind that if someone is bringing more stress than good into your life, then you should probably move along. But there is nothing like tragedy to bring people together. Right when the firings started, we began texting each other. After all, we were the only people who could understand what we were going through. What we went through was so traumatizing that it made all of our past friendship issues seem like nothing. It was more important to be there for each other than to hold on to grudges. There was no conversation about the past, we just let it go.

The Tough-Love Friend with a Heart of Gold: I remember when everything started to go down, Katie Maloney and Taylor Strecker were constantly calling to update me. I was too scared to check social media, and they would let me know what was being said. There were a few times we got into little arguments because they were urging me to handle the situation the way *they* thought I should. I knew they meant well and were looking after me, but it's easy to *tell* someone what to do when you're not the one in the situation. My life was going up in flames, not theirs. I appreciated that they didn't sugarcoat anything. They were holding me accountable, and at the same time I felt so much love and support from them. Especially since all the trolls were calling for them to denounce me as a friend. So get yourself an honest AF friend who cares.

The Shoulder to Cry On: For me this was Beau. I get this is a "friends" list, but your husband is supposed to be your BFF, right? That man let me sob and wail and snot all over him. Most of his T-shirts were covered in wet mascara and bronzer streaks for months. I was really lucky in that I had a lot of friends who constantly checked up on me and let me sob through the phone, but this was at the height of Covid, so Beau truly was all I had at home with me every day. He had to hold me like a baby twenty thousand times. I can't imagine what being canceled would've been like if I hadn't been with him and his comfy shoulder. Everyone needs a BFF who will let them sob and snot on their shoulder.

The Encourager: I want to shout out my assistant, Lo, who is also my friend. She didn't quit when everyone else did. It wasn't in her best interest to stand by someone who may never work again, but she did. And on top of that, she was always there with the most encouraging words, texts, and emails. Anytime she saw I was upset, she knew exactly what to say to make me feel like I was going to power through and be okay. It meant the world to feel like I had someone who still believed in me when it wasn't the popular thing to believe in me. Encouragers are key when you're at rock bottom and need a boost.

The Ones You Didn't Expect: I've always talked about how on *Vanderpump Rules*, our crew became our family. When I hit rock bottom and got fired, so many of my producers were more there for me than some of my own family members. And they had no reason to be: I had just been let go by the network, after all. One of them even came with me to my first pregnancy ob-gyn appointment. It meant the world to me. I had always considered them such great friends, but it wasn't until I was fired that I realized they also felt the same. When you're at a low, you'll be surprised not only by who ghosts you but also by who lifts you up. Remember the ones who lift you up.

CHAPTER 2

Sober AF

s fate would have it, at a time when I could have really used some cocktails or several bottles of pinot grigio, I was pregnant and couldn't drink. Well, I *could* have, like a fabulous French woman who sips rosé at her ultrasound appointments, but I chose not to. I was canceled, I lost my jobs (plural), and I was sober AF.

During that time, I had to get seriously creative to deal because all my normal coping mechanisms were off-limits. Normally when I got canceled or broken up with, I just turned to booze and Xanax and called it a day. I'm not proud of that, and I don't recommend that to anyone (even French women), but this book is about honesty, and in the past I 100 percent abused Xanax and alcohol when I've gone through tough times. I wish I could say that baked goods or a hard-core knitting session helped me bounce back, but that would be a massive lie. Although, while

I was pregnant, I did develop a mild baking addiction, but more on that later.

In *Next Level Basic* I wrote about my tactics for coping with breakups. During a difficult time I would usually allow myself to feel the pain, and I would self-medicate, get out of town, go get drunk at Neiman Marcus and go shopping, and then buy myself a breakup present. Being pregnant during a crisis means self-medicating is off-limits, unless you're self-medicating with Sour Patch Kids, salt-and-vinegar chips, and Cinnamon Toast Crunch. (TBH, those things actually did help.)

I could allow myself to feel the pain I was feeling, but I couldn't let it consume me. I had a baby to grow, and I didn't want any stress affecting even one of her eyelashes. I tried to get out of town, but with Covid, at that time the only places I could go were all naturey and isolated, and that's not really my vibe, especially when it comes to boosting my mood. Going to Paris was off-limits, and the thought of staying on a lake or in the woods didn't really lift my spirits. I couldn't get drunk at Neiman's because of the whole nondrinking thing, and also the pandemic again. I also definitely wasn't buying myself a present because I had just gotten fired from all my jobs, so . . . yeah.

I fantasized about margaritas my entire pregnancy. I remember the day I decided to take a pregnancy test. It was May 2, 2020, a mere three days before Cinco de Mayo. I woke up and told Beau that I was going to take a test since I was two days late, and his response was "Can't you just wait until after Cinco de Mayo so you can have margaritas with me?" He's a supes supportive partner. I told him I would wait to take a test, just to appease him, but then I snuck down into the bathroom and took three tests behind his back. What can I say? I'm impatient. Needless to say, I didn't get to celebrate Cinco de Mayo, and Beau never lets me forget it.

Since I was stuck being sober AF, I had to come up with new ways to deal with heartache that involved nonalcohol-related, stay-at-home activities. Here are some of the things that got me through:

Watching *Outlander*: Boy, did *Outlander* serve as a freaking *phenom* distraction. When I get depressed, I need a show that I can become fully invested in. Like, I wouldn't dare scroll through Instagram while I was watching *Outlander*. So *that* type of show. When I watched this time-travel sci-fi love story, I didn't think about any of my real-life problems. I binged all five seasons and became obsessed during the summer of 2020. OBSESSED. So obsessed that when I finished all the seasons, I decided to just start it all over again because I wasn't ready to say goodbye. I had already suffered enough losses (my job, my reputation, and life as I had known it), and now I was supposed to suffer the end of *Outlander*? Absolutely not. If you haven't watched it, and you love period shows/historical dramas like me, GET ON IT. Jamie and Claire #4eva.

Pinterest: During my canceling, social media was off-limits since everyone hated me. I avoided Twitter and Instagram, so Pinterest made a roaring comeback. On any normal day when I'm not being canceled, I scroll through Instagram, Twitter, Facebook, and my favorite tabloid, the *Daily Mail*, all day long. I had to stop looking because any time I opened those apps, I either saw an unflattering (to say the least) article about myself or just horrible comments directed toward me. Social media became scary AF, and Pinterest became the only safe space for me to scroll. I'd never see anything bad on Pinterest! My homepage was all babies, cake hacks, and maternity OOTDs. Basically, Pinterest became my salvation and my church.

Christmas music: There is no other music that makes me feel the way Christmas music does. I should've known Beau was my soul mate the second I realized he was okay with me playing "Santa Baby" all year round. It just makes me feel so truly happy. There was *many* a night when Beau and I would listen to Christmas music while we made dinner together. If Beau saw I wasn't in the best mood, he'd make sure to quickly put on "Jingle Bell Rock" or something. It just soothes the shit out of me and makes me feel like anything is possible, like everything was going to be okay. If my baby doesn't like Christmas music, we're gonna have an issue.

Baking: I can't believe what my life has come to. Instead of drunk shopping at Neiman's, I found joy in mastering the perfect funfetti cake. As I mentioned, my Pinterest was filled with cake hacks, in particular, cake-box hacks. Why? Because I'm not a freakin' pastry chef. I still need that boxed cake mix, but I just research ways to make them better! My pregnancy cravings were all sugar. Before pregnancy, I was someone who didn't even like dessert. I wanted my wedding cake to just be stacked wheels of cheese, and my idea of dessert was a fourth slice of pizza or an after-dinner drink. So #DessertLife was very new to me. Making cakes became therapeutic. I actually discovered an amazing secret: butter extract.

Pay it forward and pass this along: we always add vanilla extract to our desserts when baking, but butter extract is where it's at. It just makes your cake taste that much better. I've become a butter extract monster; I've told all my friends about it, and it took everything in me not to go live on Instagram proclaiming my undying love for butter extract.

Fantasizing about Halloween and Christmas: I don't know if it was a weird nonfood-related pregnancy craving, or just my need to find joy somewhere, or just my love of holidays, but I thought about Halloween and Christmas 24-7. Instead of waking up and checking Instagram, I would search for holiday inspo. I think Beau had to store about seventeen boxes of Grandin Road holiday decorations in our attic in the beginning of July. Looking back, maybe I became so obsessed because I was unconsciously focusing on a period of time where I was hoping life would be happier and back to normal. Maybe by Christmas I'd have a job, the pandemic would be over, and life would be blissful again! I'm gonna have to ask my therapist about that one.

Beau: This isn't really an activity, but I know we all think our significant others are the best ever, but FOR REALS, mine actually is. You really find out a lot about someone when you lose everything. I wake up every day happy because of Beau. I felt so freaking thankful for him. I have never felt such unwavering support in my entire life. I have never seen someone want to protect me more in my entire life. And I have never felt more loved. On days I should've been crying over the demise of my career, I was crying happy tears because I couldn't believe how lucky I was to have him. And I made sure to tell him that every time I thought about it. I kept thinking about what it would've been like to go through everything single, without him, and that thought always quickly turned any anger I held into gratitude. He remained so optimistic, happy, and strong, and I'm truly grateful that rubbed off on me.

My dogs: I'm so glad my dogs can't read TMZ. I would die if they ever felt disappointed in me. While so many people were shouting at me with their pitchforks, my little pups never left my side. When I became pregnant, Refund became absolutely obsessed with me. At first, Beau and I thought that she had just become extra needy because she had gotten used to us being home quarantining for months. But it was only me she would religiously follow around. I couldn't even go to the bathroom without her shadowing me. Beau googled it one day and saw that some dogs react that way when a woman becomes pregnant, and that just melted my cold little heart.

My baby: As I've said, I couldn't allow myself to really freak out because I wanted to keep my baby healthy and stress-free. But that's not the only way she helped. When I was canceled, I had a lot of people checking in on me, and I felt like everyone was expecting me to be depressed and losing my mind, but for the most part, as down as I was, I was also the happiest I had ever been. I was so overjoyed to be pregnant that my focus and attention was always on the little creature growing inside my belly. I read all those bogus news articles about me checking into a hospital because of a mental/emotional breakdown and shook my head. I was okay; I was good. Of course I was devastated and upset, but I also spent so much of my time reassuring everyone not to worry about me. My baby also saved me in that she kept me sober and clearheaded. Katie Maloney asked me if I thought I would've handled it all differently had I not been pregnant, and at first I wasn't sure. But then I realized, I would have totally Dark Passenger–ed everyone around me, 24-7. I would have turned to my trusted wine, and I would've spiraled. I was meant to be pregnant throughout that time, because instead of getting angry and irrational, I was able to work through it in a clearheaded, healthy way, by thinking about my baby and consuming large amounts of cake. My daughter saved me.

Taking classes: I can joke all day about distracting myself with Halloween decorations and Betty Crocker cake recipes, but in all seriousness, the classes I took, the books I read, the research I did to educate myself made all the difference. When you're canceled, it is so easy to get angry and feel like a victim. Every time my Zoom class ended, I felt lighter. I felt like I was actually doing something that could contribute good to the world. It also helped me better understand why I was canceled. Educating myself erased any anger I felt, which helped me move on and try to become better.

Prayers of freakin' gratitude: Another bullet point that I can't believe I'm writing. Did you ever think I'd be talking about prayers of gratitude?! Who am I?! I'm still the same basic bitch, just a little more evolved, I guess. Hear me out. Any time I felt scared for the future or sad about what happened, I would sit quietly and just thank God for everything I do have. And this was all new, because I've never been a religious or spiritual person. I mean, I love Ouija boards and the occult, but I've always been one of those people who only prays to God when I'm hungover and don't want to vomit. *Please God, if you make my nausea go away, I will make any deal you want.* Yeah, I'm that girl. But being at rock bottom truly just made me realize how much I still had. I have been totally freaking blessed. And I spent so much time praying and thanking God for Beau, for my family, my friends, my baby, my house, and the fact that I was able to work so much before getting fired. I was thankful for every Khaleesi who believed I could learn and be better, thankful I at least got to tour when I did, thankful I've traveled to so many places. Thankful I'm healthy, that my loved ones are healthy. The next time you go through a tragedy, I really urge you to focus on what you do have. It truly brings everything into perspective.

So sobriety is not my preferred lifestyle, but I will say I've never felt more clearheaded and focused. And I truly loved never being hungover. The Dark Passenger—that irrational, out-of-control person I used to become when drunk—was nowhere to be found. I hate to admit this, but sometimes I feel like sobriety suits me. I'm just always in a happy mood, and I'm so levelheaded. It's way harder to rattle me when I'm sober. That could also be the baby though. And as much as I enjoyed the sober pregnant life, I still counted the days until I could day-drink Aperol spritzes all day long. I fantasized about my first post-baby cocktail more than I fantasized about the end of quarantine.

COPING MECHANISMS
PRE-PREGNANCY

BIG A F BOTTLE OF WINE

PINOT GRIGIO

A FEW HAPPY PILLS

PREGNANT COPING MECHANISMS

MORE BAKING IDEAS

YOU'RE WELCOME

BUTTER EXTRACT

CUPCAKES FOR DAYS

Rock-Bottom TAKEAWAY

As fabulous as it sounds to sip rosé until you give zero fucks, I can now say that my nine months of sobriety were good for my mental health, and for my baking skills. I found healthier coping mechanisms, like making Yule log cakes or listening to Christmas music in July, and I discovered that keeping my shit together and not sinking into a dark, pinot-fueled rage actually suited me. I'm sure it was better for Beau too, even though he missed having a wife to drink margaritas with. I guess my main takeaway is that now instead of turning straight to a bottle of wine when things go south, I might have a *glass* of wine, bake a cake, watch a show, and then fall asleep because I'm exhausted from feeding a baby all night. I'll take that over crying into a wine bottle on national TV any day.

CHAPTER 3

Water Works

I have always been a firm believer in the life-changing power of a good sob session.

In other words, I am very much here for crying. In fact, I am an Olympic-champion-level weeper. I can cry over almost anything. It's not just normal shit that sets me off, like when babies are born, or at weddings, or because of death, or when old people are sweet, or when I see an old person fall, or if I'm being broken up with, or if I have to leave my dogs for a trip. I have sometimes cried on vacation just because I felt so lucky to be on an awesome trip drinking an Aperol spritz looking at an old building in Italy or something. I look forward to the day when I can go on vacation again and cry, this time because I'm so overjoyed that the pandemic is over and we can travel again and sit in public places without a mask and emote.

Sometimes I cry during horror movies when I get scared. I cry when it's my birthday, or if I'm angry, or if I'm happy and having the best time ever. I can look at a rainbow and cry. I can probably cry over a Progressive insurance commercial. Basically, anything you can think of triggers me. Crying is a release for me, and I am all about it. Big fan. Huge.

But, like many of you, in 2020 my weeping went to a whole new level, for many reasons. And it wasn't always a fun, healthy cry. Sometimes it just sucked.

It all started on January 1, 2020, as soon as the clock struck midnight. Seriously. I had the worst migraine on New Year's Eve and didn't want to go out, but, thanks to Beau's FOMO, I forced myself. When I got home just after midnight, my head wasn't any better, and sometimes the only way to ease the agony of a migraine is to cry it out, so I did. My first cry of 2020 was painful. Like, my head was actually killing me. I should've known the year was doomed. How did I not see the signs?!

After that, 2020 was great—until it became the Year of the Ugly Sob. The Year from Hell. The Year We All Cried a Bajillion Tears While Alone at Home. I mean, I was experiencing howling, weeping convulsion-like sobs. 2020 left no room for whimpers or pretty cries. If it wasn't a good wail, it might as well have never happened. Because I went through so many intense crying sessions when I hit rock bottom, I got a lot of the sobbing out of my system by about July. My remaining cries were reserved for sentimental baby stuff—mini infant UGGs or the Harry Potter mobile my mom made for the baby. I went through so much hell; in some ways it made me stronger, and now it's harder to rattle me. I mean, who *didn't* cry during Covid? Whether you were scared or frustrated or bored to death, I feel like everyone cried at least once in 2020. And if it was just once, you're very lucky, or heavily medicated.

It's not just migraines and tragedy and rainbows that make me weep. I cry when I see famous people too. I remember the first time I saw fashion designer/entrepreneur Rachel Zoe. It was right after I filmed season one of *Vanderpump*, and I was at lunch with Katie and Kristen at a restaurant called Hugo's. I was obsessed with Rachel Zoe all through high school and college, so I started crying at the table when I spotted her. My friends were totes confused and were like, "What the fuck is wrong with you?" I said I couldn't explain it, that I was just feeling overwhelming emotion because Rachel Zoe was at the next table. It just overtook me, and the emotions and tears started pouring out of me. I didn't approach her in tears though, so I do have some restraint.

Honestly, it's hard to think of times when I don't cry. There are so many, I'm going to break them into groups for you:

Work

In her book *Bossypants*, Tina Fey writes: "Some people say 'Never let them see you cry.' I say, if you're so mad you could just cry, then cry. It terrifies everyone." I am so here for this, and here's why: crying is a great way to get what you want, but then again it is also a double-edged sword. I'm not here to say don't cry at work or cry at work. I'm here to say that you need to master the art of crying at work, and use it wisely. Know when to let it loose, and when to reel it in.

Think about it: What happens when someone cries at work? Everyone is taken aback, there is nothing you can say, and it shuts down arguments because people are so freaked out that someone is crying. People take your feelings way more seriously than they did before you let the tears flow, because they go into fight-or-flight mode and they're like, *This person is really sad, so I'm going to help them / I'm going to run away.* Either way, crying might help you get what you want, but don't become that annoying bitch people are scared to be around because she is always crying. People get annoyed if you are constantly crying, and then it becomes more like "Okay, Brenda, go home. This is so annoying and we can't get anything done here." You don't want to be Brenda, so you need to be able to handle your shit. It's all about knowing when to pull the crying card and when to shut it off. It's a subtle art.

A lot of my crying-at-work practice happened at SUR. I have cried in every single corner of that place. It's obscene. Every bathroom stall at SUR is painted with my tears. I would get texts from a guy I was dating at the time, and I would be so upset that I would walk away from a table I was serving mid-order to go cry behind the coffee bar, or I would run into the kitchen and huddle in a corner in the fetal position and sob. Totally profesh. The owners had to drag me out of that kitchen many times. I think being on reality TV actually fueled my crying, because I would get rewarded if I cried while filming a scene because inevitably the tears would be what would wind up on TV. I don't mean rewarded like they'd hand me a treat, but I *would* get more screen time, which, back then, made me feel like I'd accomplished something.

Despite the rewards I reaped for crying on national television, all that crying *can be* embarrassing at times. I like to think I've outgrown it, and that I'm entering a new phase where crying on TV to get what I want is not one of my job skills. When I'm sober crying, I think I'm a pretty crier, but when I'm drunk crying? I'm heinous. I look like Gollum's mom. I'm slurring, I'm blotchy, my makeup is smeared, my psoriasis is showing. It's not ideal. Crying at work or *because* of work had its benefits for me in the past, but I hope to not cry anymore *because* of work. My work-related cries in 2020 were so loud and unhinged, I'm pretty sure my neighbors heard me wailing. Actually all of Beachwood Canyon probably heard these cries. I think my dogs even ran away downstairs a few times to huddle together. It wasn't a good look, or a good sound.

Relationships

As far as relationships go, luckily Beau is not scared of my crying, and he doesn't shut down or get annoyed if he sees tears (at least, not always). Like work situations, crying helps me when Beau and I argue because when I start crying he automatically stops being angry with me, since he feels for me and wants to talk it out, and he becomes loving and comforting. I have used this weapon to make a fight stop, 100 percent. I have also dated guys who loathed my cries, so it didn't work with them. But it works with Beau. I don't think of it as manipulating him; I see it as expressing emotion in a profound way so that he'll stop being angry and we can make up and go back to watching TV together.

I firmly believe that more men should cry. It's sexy. In fact, I don't know any women who don't find it sexy. Whenever I've seen Beau cry, his tears end the argument because I just want to comfort him. I live for it. I don't want him to be sad, but it's like *You're so in touch with your emotions as a man that you're allowing this to happen!* I'm so here for it. Men don't even understand how manipulative they could be if they cried more. They are not using their power or the tools. If more men cried, the amount of fights would decrease by a million. If your boyfriend wanted to have a guys night and you got mad and he started crying, you would be like, "Oh my God, go out for a week!" He could do whatever he wanted if he just cried. Within reason, obvs.

By far the most embarrassing crying episode I've ever experienced happened after Patrick and I broke up (please note that most of my most painful/embarrassing stories involve this guy). I took all my sadness and frustration and channeled it into . . . Instagram. After that breakup, I filmed myself for *months*, and the filming usually involved me crying into my phone and posting the videos to social media. To this day I still go to meetings where people are like, "When you documented your breakup it was so entertaining!" I usually answer with something like, "That's nice. . . ." I mean, I look back on that time and those videos and I want to vomit. What was I thinking? What people should have said at the time was, "Get this chick a tranquilizer and confiscate her phone because she is embarrassing AF."

With Beau, thankfully I don't feel the need to get so dramatic. When I go to Beau and tell him something is bothering me, and then I walk to our bedroom for some "alone time," I know he is going to ultimately follow me in there, so it helps to cry so that he finds me in there and knows I mean business. It's way more effective than anger. He always responds to tears over anger, so try it for yourself and thank me later when your significant other follows you into the bedroom to see if you need a massage or a glass of wine or some chocolate.

Crying is a talent. And as with every talent, you need to practice and learn how to control and hone your craft. If you learn how to wield it properly, it will become an important tool in your toolbox at work, in relationships, or even with customer service reps. You can't just use the hammer though, meaning you can't *always* just full-on cry. Sometimes you have to use the wrench or a chisel, meaning maybe throw in a pout here and there, or a sniffle, or just get to the *verge* of tears with a quivering lip or something. Like I said, it takes discipline, and a lifetime of practice, which I have.

Revenge

Crying in public is a very effective tool if you want to get back at someone and embarrass them. I highly recommend it. This is particularly useful when your significant other has just treated you like crap. Cry in public to embarrass/shame them! Make sure it's a crowded place. Everyone will stare and shoot him or her looks of disgust. I've actually gotten free drinks when I've used this tactic, because people feel so bad for me. My ex would leave the scene, and I would stay behind, getting sympathy and cocktails from bartenders and total strangers. It's the best revenge.

Pregnancy/Parenthood

Pregnancy crying is so satisfying! One day when I was reading one of my pregnancy books, I was imagining seeing my future baby's little face for the first time and thinking about what it would be like when I first got to do skin-to-skin with her, and I started crying. Like, what? It was just me imagining her, all covered in gross blood and white goop, and I still cried? Like, how am I going to be able to actually look at her face when she comes out? I'm not going to be able to handle it. I loved to scroll through my Instagram search section (which quickly became all things baby related) and just watch baby video after baby video and tear up for hours. I especially loved to sit in her nursery and get misty. I just sat there and stared at the little baby toys and blankets and crib and the tears rolled down my face. When I see father-daughter videos, that's it. Imagining Beau and Baby H together was just too much for me to handle. Ironically enough, as I was writing this, I was testing out a waterproof mascara for when I went to the hospital, because I knew I'd be weeping all over the place but I also wanted to look halfway decent. UPDATE: I cried when Hartford was born (duh); I cried when I stared into her eyes in the hospital; I cry when she naps because I'm not with her; I cry when she cries. As a mom, I'm basically always in tears.

Rock-Bottom TAKEAWAY

Crying to help pull yourself out of rock bottom? HIGHLY. REC-OMMEND. I mean, that's truly one of the only ways to feel and process pain, at least for me. I personally believe that's why I can bounce back so quickly from sadness. I sit in that sorrow, I digest it, I really cry it out . . . and then it's over. I guess crying is my path to closure. It's my way of feeling, processing, acknowledging, and then moving on all at once. It takes so much out of a person to have a good hard cry that of course you're not going to want to do it again. Once it's done, it's done. So the next time you find yourself at rock bottom, don't try to be all tough and stoic, because you're only pro-longing the inevitable. Just feel it, digest it, and cry it the eff out.

PLACES STASSI HAS CRIED
(THERE ARE MANY)

SUR

EVERY INCH OF THIS PLACE

SUNSET BLVD.
CRESCENT HEIGHTS

MANY A PUBLIC STREET CORNER

MY CAR

BATHROOM STALLS ACROSS WEST HOLLYWOOD

Stassi's Best and Worst Movie and TV Cries

✳ **Kim Kardashian:** Anytime Kim K has cried on TV, I am equal parts amused, moved, and entertained. I laugh and feel for her simultaneously. Her lack of wrinkles when she emotes also makes me want to run and get my Botox touched up.

✳ *The Room:* If you haven't seen the cult classic movie *The Room*, stop reading this book immediately and take a break to watch this literal piece of art (but then come back to the book). The main character Johnny's pitiful crying scenes are pure comedy and deeply satisfying to watch.

✳ *The NeverEnding Story:* When Atreyu's horse dies?! I mean, are you kidding me putting that into a kids' movie? It's scarring, truly scarring, in a good way.

✳ Cameron Diaz in *The Holiday:* One of my past bosses used to always tell me that I reminded him of Cameron Diaz's character in *The Holiday.* I never totally understood that because her character is incapable of crying, so how does that match my dramatic-ass personality? Anyway, I always loved the end of the movie when she finally cries! That moment gives me all the feels.

✳ *Something's Gotta Give:* I get that Diane Keaton is supposed to be funny and over the top in this extremely dramatic-crying montage, but it drives me crazy. I love this movie, I love Diane, but it's so annoying. It's a terrible cry, and I should know.

✳ *Forrest Gump*: I won't spoil it if you haven't seen the movie (in which case, *who are you?)* but the end scene just breaks me. It's one of the best cries in movie history, IMO.

✳ *The Bachelor* (first episode, night one, every single season): Every season without fail, after the rose ceremony on the first night, there's always a handful of axed contestants who cry over being let go, and it's amazing. Like, you guys have literally been there for only a few hours, you barely know the Bachelor, so why the hell are you crying?! It's truly fantastic to watch.

✳ *Signs*: Okay, in *Next Level Basic*, I wrote about my love of M. Night Shyamalan movies, especially *Signs*. This movie also has one of the most intense crying scenes I've ever seen. A lot of people hate it, but I feel like it's powerful AF. You know that scene toward the end where the whole family is sitting down to have their sort of "last meal" situation? The kids start crying along with Mel Gibson. There is something so freaking compelling about a father crying because he's scared for his children. That scene gets me every damn time. Like, I can't.

✳ *Moulin Rouge!*: In *Next Level Basic*, I also talked about my obsession with *Moulin Rouge!*, which also coincidentally has a *supes* intense crying scene. It's when Satine dies in the end, which is not a spoiler, since they tell you that from the very beginning, so calm down. Anyway, when she dies, Ewan McGregor's character, Christian, is like totally inconsolable, snot dripping from his mouth, just screaming and wailing all over her dead body. Some people might think it's over the top, but all I know is that's exactly what Beau better be like when I pass away, otherwise I'm coming back to haunt his ass.

✳ *Dumbo*: Okay, now that I am a mother, this really hits home. I used to listen to "Baby Mine" and weep all the time when I was pregnant. This scene shouldn't be allowed in a movie, it's so sad. Dumbo just wants to be with his freaking mom, and they're hugging with their trunks while she is locked away. Even as I am typing this, I'm starting to choke up. I am not, nor will I ever be, emotionally stable enough to handle this scene.

CHAPTER 4

End of an Era: Au Revoir, Vanderpump

I should have read the signs.

In May 2020, one of the *Vanderpump Rules* editors went on a podcast and spilled the tea about how the show works behind the scenes. She peeled back the curtain of reality TV and her comments went semi-viral, and not in a good way, so I would imagine she got in major trouble. One of the things she said involved me and Beau, and it was something about us being "heroes" of the show or something, which led to anti-Stassi fans of the show and certain cast members hating me more than they already did. They thought a "hero edit" meant that the producers would make me look good no matter what, which, if you've seen the show, you know is laughable. A "hero edit" actually means that Beau and I had to be in every episode. I would not say I was ever edited to look *good*. If that were the case, would I come across as so unlikable to so many people?

Vanderpump is all about drama, and I filmed plenty of scenes over the years that never aired because there's no juicy conflict if I'm having lunch with a friend and everything goes just *fine*. If Tom Sandoval hadn't tried to ruin my book signing in season eight, that never would have aired. The producers didn't even want to film the Witches of WeHo wine event I had with Kristen and Katie until they found out we weren't getting along. And guess what? I looked like a total bitch in that scene! There was nothing heroic about it. I was committed to putting it all out there on camera and not holding back, and it made for good TV. Looking back, though, that podcast where the editor spilled the tea was nothing compared to what came next. Once I was canceled, getting called out for "hero edit" drama was almost cute.

For nearly a decade, *Vanderpump Rules* was my life. It was my job, my circle of friends, and a chronicle of my twenties. Can you imagine if all the things you did in your twenties had been documented for the world to see, on Bravo? All the good times and bad, the drunken fights, the exes, the drama. It might sound awful to some, but it was all I knew, and I loved it.

But now it's over, at least for me.

I remember the first scene I ever filmed for *Vanderpump Rules*, back in 2013, more clearly than any other scene since—even my engagement scene. It was the one where, dead serious, I said my now infamous line to my then boyfriend Jax, "I am the devil, and don't you forget it." This is basically how the Bravo-watching world was introduced to me: as a stone-cold basic bitch. I'm proud of that. It was a title I carried with pride for many years.

When I first found out I was going to be on this new show, I was so incredibly excited to start filming. I felt like I was living my best life, like Lauren Conrad on *The Hills*. I had Pinterested outfit ideas for my first scene for months before we started shooting. That intro look was so important to me, it was like my coming-out debutante outfit! I wanted to do my hair in a high slicked-back ponytail so the focus would be on my face. Classic. Then I found a little baby-doll dress that I figured would be perfect. It was white, so I could trick people into thinking I was angelic. It was roomy, so I could eat whatever I wanted and not have to worry about sucking in. And it was short, so I could show off my legs—the one part of my body that never seemed to fluctuate no matter how much ranch dressing and pizza and wine I consumed.

I paired this outfit with a gorgeous vintage statement necklace I found at a flea market. When I put it all together, I felt timeless. And honestly, mission accomplished, because I would still wear that exact outfit today. I remember getting our call time, meaning the time we were expected to show up on set. It was me, Jax, Katie, Kristen, and Tom Sandoval, and we were going to go have brunch at a place called Tart. Jax drove there with me and Katie in my old Toyota Camry Solara convertible. God I loved that car. Jax and I were already fighting before we got to Tart, because that's what we did. We fought. Before production even began I knew that Jax and I were heading for splitsville. We never got along, and the fights we had were epic, meaning epically disastrous. We had the most toxic relationship you could possibly imagine. The night before our first scene, Jax didn't even come home, so who knows where he had slept. It was not good. I told myself there was no way I was going to film a public breakup for this new reality show, so my plan was to wait it out and break up after filming was over.

It's always funny when people have a "plan" going into a reality show, because it never works out the way you expect it to. In fact, it normally ends up the exact opposite of what you expect. That said, of course we have to plan certain things. I mean, the crew didn't just show up at our door, yell "Surprise!," and start filming. At one point I did (briefly) take up spin classes, and you have to plan to film those things and get permission and set up cameras. Actually, the crew *does* show up unannounced sometimes. Like in season one, there was a scene where I went to a club with Frank (ew) and left with Jax (ew again) because Jax showed up and convinced me how much he loved me *blah blah blah*. The next morning, my friend Jennifer Bush (who was also at the club) texted me that after I left, Frank told her that Jax had cheated on me in Las Vegas. Jax wasn't there, so I was alone in the shitty apartment we shared. I started sobbing and literally vomiting after hearing that he'd cheated. I was supposed to work a lunch shift at SUR that day, and I called crying, telling them that there was no way I could show up because I had just found out Jax cheated on me. Well, our producers found out that I was having a meltdown, so they sent the crew to my apartment to cover my rock-bottom heartbreak moment as it was going down. I had no idea they were going to come barging into my apartment. I had no makeup on; I was sobbing and was puffy.

It was so real and raw because I was so unprepared, and everything was happening in real time. That's the scene where I drank a shit ton of Jax's Cristal champagne out of Solo cups because it felt like revenge.

Production also barged in unannounced every single morning on every cast trip I ever went on. Our producers had keys to our hotel rooms, and they came in while we were sleeping so they could film us waking up. It's a major mind fuck (I mean, would you want to wake up with a professional camera crew in your hungover face?), and I've had nightmares about it. Now that I'm fired, I legit miss that though. I would actually pay a large amount of money to go on a cast trip in Mexico and have our crew sneak into my hotel room while I'm hungover and still sleeping, looking like shit. Compared to being canceled and unemployed, it sounds like a dream.

Ever since the first season of *Vanderpump*, when my life didn't play out the way I expected it to at all, I realized I would never try to plan anything ever again when it came to plot or story. I would go into every season blind, and let things happen. That decision totally made filming a show for eight years much easier, since I could just act normal instead of stressing about what I thought should happen. Being on reality TV is a good lesson for letting things just unfold in everyday life, actually, which is kind of ironic.

But back to that first scene. We all sat down, and I was so thrilled to be getting our brunch paid for that I was double-fisting and ordering drinks one after the next like it was my last meal on earth. I believe I was mixing sauvignon blanc with mimosas. I mean, we were genuinely broke at the time! I had to use the opportunity to eat and drink all I could, because who knew how long it would last. That whole lunch consisted of me and Jax going at each other's throats, in between ladylike sips of my drink. I felt so bad for my friends because they were just exhausted by all of it and could hardly get a word in. I remember leaving that scene and saying to the producer, "This is going to be a really boring show if it's just about me and Jax fighting all the time." I guess the joke was on me, because it turns out, that was exactly what that season would be about, and it was exactly what made it so addicting for people, seeing me and Jax tear each other apart emotionally. Obviously we eventually broke up, and other dramas took place (so many dramas), and for eight years *Vanderpump Rules* kind of defined me. I got to work with my closest friends on that show, and then, like I said, in what felt like a flash, it was over.

Despite being called old by the newer, younger cast in my last seasons, I still loved doing the show. Plus, it was my job, it paid my rent and bills. I know I wasn't working in a coal mine or an ER, but it was still my livelihood, to a large extent. Even before I was fired though, I was starting to feel like I'd outgrown it, like it didn't mirror my actual life. I hadn't worked at SUR for six years, and Lisa hadn't been my boss in ages. I wasn't going out to clubs anymore, I had met Beau, I got pregnant, and my life had truly changed. There was not going to be a scene with a pregnant Stassi throwing drinks at new cast members and telling people she was the devil. That ship had sailed away on a swift-moving river of pinot grigio, or breast milk, or both.

Before the firing, season eight was actually supposed to be my last official season of *Vanderpump Rules*. Our producers had spent the year finding a way to branch off the original cast, which I'm pretty sure Lisa Vanderpump didn't even know about. Like me, most of my friends were just outgrowing the show. We weren't the same kids who started almost a decade before. I was twenty-two when we started filming. I was getting wasted every night, dancing on tables. I was broke, and what little money I did have, I spent at happy hour. We were living our lives like we had nothing to lose, because we were broke and actually had nothing to lose except maybe our tip money. So eight years in we were all settling down, buying houses, and getting married. I mean, I wouldn't be caught dead at a club now. Honestly, the bouncer probably wouldn't even let me in. He'd take one look at me and laugh, like that scene in *Knocked Up* when pregnant Katherine Heigl tries to get past the velvet rope. I hope I'll still go out for drinks or maybe a mimosa brunch when I'm a mom, but a club just sounds like hell on earth to me now. I'd rather watch *Emily in Paris* or *Bridgerton* and eat a baguette or some crumpets in bed.

The new people on the show (mainly Dayna, Danica, and Max) were young and reckless, the same way we were when we started, and they were the future of *Vanderpump Rules*. The plan was for the original cast to eventually spin off into some sort of TBD *Valley Rules*–type show, since Kristen, Katie, Tom, Jax, Brittany, Tom, and Ariana were *all* living in the Valley. A spin-off seemed like an even better idea since the reaction to season eight was . . . not good. The audience was confused by the new characters and plots, as was I, as was our cast. It was strange just having to pretend to integrate with all these random new people that I had nothing in common with. It was also hard watching all these new people come in acting like they owned the show—a show that us OG cast members built with our blood, sweat, and tears for eight years. Fine, maybe we weren't building houses for the needy with our bare hands or working on an oil rig in the middle of the ocean, but believe it or not, we did work hard! Like I said, the new cast members constantly referred to us as old and boring (which is probably accurate, TBH) and it made the filming experience a little unpleasant. It wasn't the same *Vanderpump* anymore.

So the *Vanderpump* spin-off was supposed to be bridged by an episode about my gorgeous Italian wedding, which would then introduce the new show—surprise! We were all so looking forward to that. When Bravo announced that Kristen and I were being let go in the spring of 2020, obviously things changed. At first we thought our spin-off would still go ahead with some sort of focus on the Canceling and our journeys to educate ourselves. After all, Bravo's official statement had been that we were let go from *Vanderpump Rules*; they didn't say we were let go from Bravo. Well, we were wrong. Any hope we had slowly faded when we realized that, while we did deserve punishment, Bravo severed all ties with us, which was painful. I do get why they felt like they needed to let us go, but it still hurt. Now that time has passed and I've been able to think about all that happened, I don't harbor any resentment. That's the thing about rock bottom—in a weird way it makes you less bitter. It makes you want to understand what went wrong so it won't happen again.

When I was fired, besides being distraught and scared and hurt, I also felt a small sense of relief, because had our spin-off not gotten picked up, I don't think I would have had the courage to leave *Vanderpump Rules* on my own. Not only was the money too hard to leave but I also loved the *Vanderpump* family. We had most of the same producers and crew for eight years, and I loved each of them. My producers have been some of the most supportive people surrounding me during the hardest times in my adult life. It's funny to think that the very people whose jobs it is to manipulate and edit you on TV can end up being the ones who are there for you when you need them the most. Their friendships meant everything to me, even after I was let go. When you're at rock bottom, you really find out who truly cares about you and who truly believes in you. As I mentioned, one of my producers even came with me to my first post-firing gynecologist baby appointment. Talk about loyalty. Beau couldn't come because the Covid restrictions were tight at that time, and this producer had the same doctor as me, so she just made an appointment at the same time as mine so she could be there, since I had so much anxiety about being alone and having paparazzi follow me. I will never forget that kindness, and how much that meant to me. Saying goodbye to the crew and producers was the hardest part of the entire firing scandal. But, as much as the show meant to me, it was time. I needed to move on and figure out what else I wanted to do with my life. I didn't have the guts to do it, so Bravo did it for me.

I don't want to sound ungrateful. I can be grateful for Bravo and angry at Bravo all at the same time. *Vanderpump* gave me some of the best years of my life. Despite the drama, I have the absolute fondest memories of it, and I will always cherish those times. Maybe one day, I'll be back to reality TV. I'm only interested in reality TV that is just that . . . reality. Not this semi-real, semi-fake version of reality TV that isn't an actual reflection of what my life looks like. Do people want to see a show about breastfeeding and baby spit-up? My guess is . . . maybe? Judging from the moms and dads who love hearing about newborn life on Instagram or on our podcast *The Good the Bad the Baby*, maybe a show full of diapers and spit-up is just what reality TV needs.

If the spin-off show would've happened and if it had been well received by fans, I could have gone on forever filming it because I believe that what makes a show worth doing is who you're doing it with. And this way, I'd be continuing on with my group of friends, my chosen family. I would've never quit something like that! I think once I was let go, people were surprised to see me still constantly hanging out with Jax, Brittany, Kristen, Katie, Lala, Tom, and Randall. I think a lot of people assumed our friendship wasn't that rooted and deep, and that when the show was over and all was said and done, we would drift apart. That couldn't be further from the truth. You can't just break friendships up by firing one of us. We chose to have children at the same time so we could all grow together. We also made this pregnancy pact so no one would have FOMO. Despite everything we go through, this core group always sticks together, and I would've been in a show about that for forever.

Obviously, though, that's not happening. . . .

Even though I loved doing the show, it wasn't all cocktails and pool parties. The audience and fans were amazing, for the most part (thanks for watching, y'all), but if you're putting yourself out there, you're always going to have to deal with some haters. Like the people who tweeted that I was "in on" my proposal, which was filmed for the show. Um, I wouldn't have worn Daisy Duke cutoff shorts to my freaking proposal. I mean, my top was amazing (black-and-white polka dots, neck bow, very chic and Parisian). But with Daisy Dukes?! It was like Audrey Hepburn on top and Jessica Simpson on the bottom. Love them both, but together they just don't feel like a duo that makes sense, especially for one of the most special moments of my life.

Had I known this was going to be a truly iconic moment in my life, I probs would've gone full Audrey Hepburn, maybe with some tailored high-waisted pants. Audrey is timeless, so you can't go wrong there. But it was *hot* outside. I mean, scalding. If it were up to me, I would've chosen to go mausoleum shopping in November, not July. Anyway, the reason I genuinely didn't know it was my proposal was because this was a scene I had planned. Yep. Despite what I said about not planning things, I planned this one scene. I lost my grandmother on the first day of filming season eight, and I remember filming a scene with Beau at my apartment a few days after we came back from her funeral. One of my favorite producers, Erin Foye, was producing our scene, and I was telling her all about my family's Schroeder mausoleum in New Orleans. Ever since I was little I've always loved cemeteries, and I've always fantasized about starting my own family mausoleum. I explained that one day

I wanted to buy a Schroeder-Clark mausoleum at the Hollywood Forever Cemetery.

Before you get judgy, I get that mausoleums sound like a bougie rich-people thing, but to me it's a New Orleans thing. Many families in New Orleans have mausoleums because the city is below sea level. I want to take that tradition with me and my family to Los Angeles. I told Foye that would be a scene I'd really like to film, because that is something I'm actually looking to do, and we decided that a scene with me looking for a mausoleum would be better than another boring setting where I'm having wine in my apartment . . . again. Beau overheard me, and just like that, my proposal was set into motion.

Beau plotted with the producers to hijack my cemetery scene. Foye told the rest of our producers to set up a scene for me to go mausoleum shopping, but the scene would actually be my proposal. So the last week of July, I got my filming schedule, and it read, "July 30, mausoleum shopping with Beau," and I thought nothing of it. This was the scene I had asked to film. So I put on my Audrey Hepburn/Jessica Simpson hybrid outfit because it was freaking hot, and I went on my way. Now, looking back, I should've known something was up, because on the way to the cemetery, Beau put on my favorite soundtrack, *The Greatest Showman*, without me even asking for it. That was a dead giveaway, but I had no clue. I thought he was just being sweet.

There are always pros and cons when it comes to filming your most precious moments. I love the fact that I got to share that moment with the public. And I love that it was shot so beautifully, like where is the Emmy Award for that scene?! There were drone shots and everything! I love that my producers and crew got to be there. The only downside to filming is that sometimes you have to redo a few things, when all you want to do is just celebrate and be in the moment. We had to kiss a few extra times so that our crew could get different shots. Another downside to filming? My producers wouldn't let me change clothes in between the cemetery and then going to Lisa's house for the engagement celebration, even though we had downtime at my apartment. *Ugh.* They were afraid it wouldn't make sense continuity-wise. I was too elated to argue with them. It still would've been nice to throw on a little black dress instead of jean shorts, but in the end, it really didn't matter. At least they let me touch up my sweaty makeup and have an Aperol spritz.

Another great thing about having these things on film is that my daughter will get to see how her father proposed. She'll get to see how her parents interacted before she was born. I feel so proud that I got to show things like what it takes to write a book—the stress of making a deadline, the photoshoot for my book cover, the book-release party at TomTom that went cray cray, even the embarrassing conversation when I asked my publisher for an extension. I'm also very proud of the moment in season four when Katie and I make up. I think falling out of friendships is very common in your twenties, and humbling oneself and making up is a hard thing for both parties to do. It was a very real raw moment with my best friend, a moment I'm so glad happened. And yes, in case you are wondering, I am not ashamed to admit that I absolutely will let my daughter watch *Vanderpump Rules*. I mean, someone has to learn from my mistakes, so please let it be her. For real, I can't wait to watch her cringe. I mean, how embarrassed will she be when she sees twenty-three-year-old Stassi crying in the SUR parking lot over Jax (who will probably be like an uncle to her). I mean, that's twisted, but I'm here for it.

Maybe I'll show *Vanderpump* to Hartford when she gets to middle school and she starts to enter the era when female friendships go cray. Maybe it'll help her feel like her own friendship dramas are nothing compared to what her mom went through. My friendship with Kristen is one that basically imploded on television. I remember, around season eight, Kristen was so unhappy in her relationship at the time, but whenever Katie and I brought it up on camera, trying to talk about something real that Kristen actually *said* she wanted to talk about on camera, she closed down and tried to act like the zen "cool girl." She even saged me in a scene, like I was some toxic witch! The "cool girl" act left Katie and me looking like two bitter shrews coming after her all the time. We got fed up, because it was impossible to be real with her. It always drove me nuts when someone wasn't being themselves on camera, because it made it impossible for the rest of us to do our jobs. When they all went back to filming after I was fired, I would hear about Katie being fed up with coming across as the resident bitch, because she was the only one being real and calling people out! God, I was jealous not to be part of the drama. I missed it.

Vanderpump was a diary of my twenties: my mess-ups, my triumphs, my relationships, my breakups, my meltdowns, all of it. Will I fast-forward over when I backhand Kristen? Probs. But it was/is my life. I don't think my twenties were all that different from anyone else's. We all embarrass ourselves at some point—my embarrassing moments just happen to be documented for my daughter to see, and hopefully learn from.

Sometimes I wonder about the future of reality TV, and especially shows like *Vanderpump*. I don't know if that Regina George *Mean Girls*–type character is as entertaining as it used to be. I don't know if season one Stassi is all that funny anymore. I mean, not gonna lie, I do miss her sometimes, but for the most part, when I look back, I cringe. I was a bratty, bossy little asshole. Season-one Stassi was not inclusive. I mean, who isn't entertained by the Regina Georges of the world, but what about when it crosses a line and becomes unfunny? That's the part I hope my daughter can learn from. It's funny to be yourself and be a badass basic bitch, but at some point you have to grow up, learn from your mistakes, stop backhanding your best friends, and check your freaking privilege.

It did hurt when I was first fired and my friends would talk about filming the show. I'd usually say something like "I love you, but too soon." I remember my first girls' night out after Hartford was born, in May 2021. I went out with Lala and Katie, and it was my first boozy girls' night out in over a year. I put on heels and false eyelashes, and it was amazing. As I drank my dirty martinis, I remember Lala and Katie talking about how they were going to start filming the new season in a few days, and instead of feeling awful about it, I felt at peace. I'd accepted it, but that didn't mean I wasn't a little sad still. Like I keep saying, I can accept things, but that doesn't mean I can't also feel angry or sad sometimes. There is nothing I can do to change what happened, so I try not to let it upset me anymore. What does make me sad is that I'll miss out on so many of my friends' life events, because the show will be filming them. Like Lala's daughter's christening, or supporting Tom Schwartz at TomTom, because cameras will be rolling. What made the show so special was that we were a real group of friends who did everything together, and now I'm missing out on so many of those things. I'm not asking for pity, I'll be fine, and it's not like I'm forbidden from seeing my friends. It's just a new phase of life, and I'm getting used to it.

On that note, here are three of the most important things I took away from my time on *VPR*.

Stassi's Top Three Vanderpump Rules

1. Be yourself: There is a power in being 100 percent yourself, no matter how flawed or eccentric. People want to relate and to feel like they aren't the only ones who act a certain way or screw up. Turns out, there's a whole lot of basic bitches out there who just want to relate to other basic bitches. Instead of being embarrassed about being called a basic bitch, the second I owned it, I felt free and I was able to connect with so many other people over the same dumb things! When people ask me for advice on how to be on a reality show, my number one answer is to always be yourself. The audience is smart, they know when you're not being authentic, and they don't like it. Don't try to be any character or stereotype you think will get you attention. People can tell if you're trying to be "the levelheaded one" or "the nice one" or even "the bitchy one." Just relax, be yourself, and handle every situation that arises the way you normally would. There is so much power that comes from just being yourself. You can't argue with honesty and authenticity. No one is exactly like you, so being your own self, messy as that might be, is the best shot you have. I can't wait to teach my daughter to own whoever she ends up being.

2. Stop being so judgy: This one may come as a surprise given that I've based a whole career off of judging, but just bear with me. When I brag about being judgy, I mean it in a funny, lighthearted way. I truly believe that being on *VPR* has made me less judgmental, because I've received so much judgment for living my mistakes out loud. I've been condemned for my screwups over and over again, and that has made me less judgmental of everyone else's low moments. Whenever I catch myself judging someone else, I always try to remind myself to think about what that person might be going through or what could have led them to make a certain decision. We never have the full story (remember Meghan and Harry's Oprah interview?!). Now, I still encourage lighthearted judging, because the world would be super bore bore without some light teasing, but I always make sure to include myself in the joke. If you're going to laugh at other people, you have to be able to laugh at yourself. I do get judgy about things like Kylie Jenner posting a back-to-school photo of her daughter carrying a $12,000 back-pack, or Jax posting yet another video of himself mowing the lawn, but those choices are harmless. I try to reserve real judgment for when I have the whole story, and being on *Vanderpump* taught me the importance of that.

3. Find your family: If you watched the show, my group of friends probably seems completely dysfunctional. I know from the outside we can seem cringey and annoying, but I love them all, and I owe that to *Vanderpump Rules*. Yes, I was friends with a lot of them before we even had a show, but the eight years we had filming and working together glued us together in a way that feels unbreakable. For example: if we hadn't had the show, I never would've spoken to Kristen or Jax again after season two. We've had so many break-ups (romantic and friend breakups) in our group of friends, and while being on the show fueled some of the biggest breakups, it also forced us back together. Now that the show is all over for me, I feel like my friendships are deeper and more cemented than before. We're starting a new generation of actual humans. We'll take family vacations together, watch each other's children while we have date nights, and do whatever grown-ass parents do together. I'm so thankful for *VPR* for giving me that.

Rock-Bottom TAKEAWAY

From the moment the cameras started rolling on *Vanderpump Rules*, I knew I had found my basic bitch calling. The show allowed me to be as loud, obnoxious, and judgy as I could be from day one, but over the years (I hope) I mellowed and grew and all those things you're supposed to do as you get older and become a better human. I don't regret that my twenties were filmed and broadcast for millions of people to see, and I gained lifelong friends (and made some lifelong enemies) in the process. Getting fired was a major blow—it was the bottom of a very rocky fall—but I learned to move on and search for new things to get excited about, like the podcast Beau and I created, or our baby, or this book. So even if you lose your dream job, or what you think is your dream job, something else will come along. I'll forever love *Vanderpump*, and the fans, and my friends. It wasn't fun losing it all, but now I can double-fist my pinot grigio in the privacy of my own home.

Stassi's Cringiest Moments on Vanderpump Rules

I know I've grown up and learned from my mistakes, and oh the mistakes I have made. That would actually be an amazing title for a musical about my life: *Oh, the Mistakes I Have Made! The Stassi Schroeder Story*. Because of this glorious track record, I figured why not take a trip down memory lane and relive some of my most regrettable moments from the show, the ones I will show my daughter and immediately say: "Don't do as I said *or* as I did!"

When I slapped Kristen: Violence is never the answer! I wish I could take it back, but I'm pretty sure this goes down in history as the slap heard 'round the world, at least the world that watches Bravo.

When I yelled at Beau in Mexico: I feel like Beau will still be giving me a hard time about this when we have grandchildren. Why couldn't I have just chilled the eff out and stopped being so controlling?! I freaked out because I wanted to go to bed and he wanted to stay out. I especially regret this from my vantage point of experiencing quarantine life and Covid, because what a precious thing it is to go outside the house! I should've just let him stay up and party as late as his little heart desired.

When I went nuts on my birthday(s): I don't even know which one is the worst. The time I ran down the streets of Hollywood crying, dressed as a dead person? The time I broke my own phone because, again, I was controlling AF? Who breaks their own phone? The time I repeated "It's my birthday" so many times that I would legit understand if someone thought I was a programmed fembot. God, I was so whiny and entitled, I don't know how I wasn't the one being slapped all the time. *Vanderpump Rules* has officially turned me off to my own birthdays. I have zero desire to celebrate them anymore, to the point where I've pretty much skipped them the last two years. It had the reverse effect on me. I'm truly scarred by my birthday montages, because of the way I acted.

Any scene with Patrick: No seriously. Any scene I had with my ex Patrick. I think season six was my best season, style-wise, but it was my absolute worst self-esteem-wise. I've mentioned this before, but I cringe thinking about any and every scene I had with him. Awful.

Any scene with Frank: See above. Same feeling.

"I don't know what I did to you but I'll take a pinot grigio": I will never understand how this moment became what it is—basically, one of the most quoted lines of the show. This was one of the first scenes I filmed when I came back from living in New York City, and I remember my producer, Jeremiah Smith, saying something like, "This is why we need you!" I was like, "Excuse me?" I truly didn't understand and still don't. I *didn't* know what I did to Scheana to make her so bitchy to me, and I *did* need a pinot grigio, sooooo . . . It's a mystery to me.

All the statement necklaces I wore: Do I need to write a goodbye love letter to these accessories? Why did I feel the need to wear a statement necklace with every single outfit in every single scene? I get that they were trendy at the time, but not trendy enough to wear 24-7. Sidenote: I've kept most of those necklaces because, as ugly as they were, they still feel somewhat iconic to me, like they belong in a Bravo museum or something. Maybe one day.

THE FIRST SEASON STASSI

ONCE TRENDY STATEMENT NECKLACE COLLECTION
PIECE 1 OUT OF TOO MANY

THIS NECKLACE WAS MOST LIKELY WORN
BY STASSI DURING A FIGHT WITH THEN
BOYFRIEND JAX TAYLOR.
est. 2012

Fifteen Songs for Rock Bottom

When I'm at rock bottom, I go through a million different feelings. Angry, sad, guilty, calm, inspired, feisty, remorseful, frustrated, exhausted, determined, hopeless, hopeful . . . you freakin' name it, I've felt it. That is why the following playlist may seem a tad all over the place. There are songs for when you want to fight back, songs for when you're devastated, songs for when you're inspired to rise up, and songs for when you just need to hear something to get you through the day without throwing yourself off the roof of your house. This is mainly a playlist for people with main-character syndrome (gotta love Gen Z for coining that one), aka people who envision themselves as the protagonist in the movie of their life. My main-character energy is next level when I'm depressed. I actually have a Spotify playlist called "Sparkly Butterfly" on my phone. I promise you, these songs help.

1. "Look What You Made Me Do" by Taylor Swift: This is the ultimate comeback song. I rode so hard for T. Swift when she came back from her Kim and Kanye feud, just guns blazing, giving zero effs. It's definitely cynical, but who doesn't feel a little cynicism when they're down?

2. "Run the World (Girls)" by Beyoncé: You want to feel empowered? Here ya go. I listened to this song before I went onstage for every single podcast show I did, but I also listened to it when I was down and out because it reminded me that women are capable of anything and that I'm a strong-ass woman.

3. "This Is Me" from *The Greatest Showman*: I get that I've always been someone who is polarizing. A lot of people just don't like me, and they love to tell me over and over again on social media. This song helps me to just . . . not care. I am who I am; I will never be able to please everyone. *When the sharpest words wanna cut me down / I'm gonna send a flood, gonna drown 'em out!* The lyrics are *everything*.

4. "Hang on Little Tomato" by Pink Martini: I play and sing this song to Hartford every morning when she wakes up. I listened to it throughout my pregnancy, especially when I found out about the hole in her heart. I hope she always remembers this song whenever she's going through a tough time.

5. "Woman" by Kesha: Another girl-power song that I listen to when I'm not only on top of my game, but also at rock bottom when I need to pick my ass up off the floor. Some songs just totally work for a range of feelings and situations.

6. "Have Yourself a Merry Little Christmas" by Frank Sinatra (or insert your personal favorite holiday song): TBH, it was really hard for me to pick *one* favorite holiday song for this playlist, there are so many good ones. I mean "All I Want for Christmas" by Mariah?!

But this one just really encapsulates the whole holiday spirit for me. I like to listen to Christmas music when I'm sad (or happy, or excited, or any emotion at all). Like I've mentioned, I feel like it reminds me of happier times.

7. "Not Afraid" by Eminem: I love Eminem. I love this song. It's angry yet uplifting. One of the first lines, *I guess I had to go to that place to get to this one*—I FEEL THAT SO HARD.

8. The *Game of Thrones* theme song: Before your eyes roll all the way back in your head, hear me out. This song represents a bunch of families fighting for control of an iron throne to rule pretty much everything. And when I hear this song, I channel that savage energy. Give it a listen the next time you need to get your fight on.

9. "Fight Song" by Rachel Platten: I mean, I'm pretty sure basic bitches everywhere clutch their pumpkin spice lattes and sing along to this song when they're down. I know I do.

10. "Not Ready to Make Nice" by the Chicks: This song got me through almost every tough time I have ever had as an adult. I think it's important to emphasize that just because you realize that you messed up and that you're at fault, you're still allowed to be angry and hurt and frustrated. There's a whole gray area that comes with being at rock bottom. This song helps me with that gray area.

11. "Love Me or Hate Me" by Lady Sovereign: This is the ultimate give zero fucks song. It's also, like, part comedy. If I were a cool hipster British chick, it would totally be my anthem. But I'm a basic bitch American ex–reality star, so . . .

12. "Walk on Water" by Eminem and Beyoncé: First of all, these two superstars together?! Secondly, this is my ultimate rock-bottom song. Like, if I could only choose one, it would be this one. If there was one song that could accurately describe everything I feel at the times I've been canceled, it's this one. I weep to this song. LITERALLY WEEP. I feel every single lyric in this song. I think that with cancel culture, people tend to forget that the people getting canceled are human beings who make mistakes just like everyone else. I get that I have to be held to a higher standard since I'm "well-known," but like Beyoncé sings, *I'm only human, just like you.*

13. "A Girl Like You" by Edwyn Collins: I'll admit it, I listen to this song when I'm driving and I need to stop being sad and convince myself I'm some badass James Bond assassin or something. It works.

14. "Praying" by Kesha: For anyone who has ever been wronged, which is literally everyone. One of the most powerful songs on this list. I get chills.

15. "Opus 36" from the *Marie Antoinette* soundtrack: Real talk, when I got canceled I would remind myself that Marie Antoinette was also canceled, so, like, maybe I was in good company? Obviously I realize she was beheaded, so her canceling was a teensy more intense than mine. But that didn't stop me from listening to the Marie Antoinette soundtrack nonstop so I could channel her energy. This is one of the instrumental songs when she realizes shit's going down. I would tell myself, if Marie can handle riding in an open carriage on the streets of Paris to her death, then I can handle this.

CHAPTER 5

How to Marry Your Fuckboy

This might defy all basic bitch logic, but I don't ever recall fantasizing about weddings or marriage until I became an adult. I never made Barbie and Ken walk down an aisle. I didn't own an American Girl doll with a wedding dress on. Maybe if Meghan and Harry had gotten married when I was a little girl I would have been a convert, but it took years for me to transform into a potential Bridezilla.

I think this is all probably because my parents got married so many times when I was growing up (not to each other). It was like they were saying "I do" for sport, and so I just never dreamed about marriage as some perfect fairy tale. All I knew was that *if* I was going to get married one day, I was very serious about doing it only once. I'm sure most people go into marriage convinced it will be their only wedding, unless they renew their vows with a big gala event, but still.

When I did slip and think about weddings over the years, it wasn't necessarily because of who I was dating. It was because of Pinterest. I would make wedding vision boards when I was bored and had nothing on TV to watch, and those are really my first memories of actually fantasizing about marriage. It was really about the clothes and shoes and accessories more than anything else. I made boards for hairstyles and makeup looks and table settings just to pass the time.

But then I met Beau. And even then, it took me a while to think about the m-word.

My dad married his fourth wife not too long ago, and my mom is going on her fourth husband. I grew up joking that they were try-ing to outdo each other with their sheer volume of marriages. Right now, they're tied. It's hard enough to date and not get ghosted, so how do you even trick that many people into marrying you?! Like, what are my parents doing that's making all these people fall in love with them?! Do you know how hard it was for me to convince Beau to marry me? And that's just one person! I can't remember one sin-gle time either of my parents tried to give me marriage advice grow-ing up. I mean, just because you've had a lot of practice at different types and lengths of marriages doesn't mean you're an authority on what makes a marriage work. Sorry, parents. I used to joke with my mom that I was actually destined for a life of multiple marriages. I figured it was in my blood or something. Can that be genetic?! So far, it's proven to be the opposite.

Pinterest boards aside, like I said, I never really had that strong of an urge to get married until I met Beau. I don't know if I was

scarred by all the constant divorcing going on when I was growing up, or the fact that all my past relationships were toxic AF, or
if I just hadn't felt ready. Beau also came from divorced parents,
and we're both convinced that's why neither of us had jumped
into getting married before. I have zero judgment when it comes
to multiple marriages, I just feel like it has to be exhausting. I'm
way too lazy to go through all of this again. If an Elizabeth Taylor
life of eight marriages is the one you're after, then go for it. Zero
judgment, other than the fact that it sounds draining, and also
WTF do you do with all your old wedding albums? Give them
to Goodwill?

When I met Beau, I was coming off my puke-inducing roller
coaster of a relationship with Patrick (let's just nickname him Manbun). Kristen had been trying to set me and Beau up for years.
Since my relationship with Manbun was so erratic and on-again-
off-again, it gave her plenty of opportunities to try. There were
about 7,364 mini breakups each year, averaging about one or two
major long-term breaks each year. So, super healthy. I had actually convinced myself that I loved that aspect of our relationship
because it allowed me so much independence and freedom. Manbun and I rarely saw each other, and when we did, it normally
turned into a fight with him storming off to his apartment and
not talking to me for five days. That's why I was able to have so
much fun girl time. I was constantly with my friends, constantly
going on girl trips, or just enjoying my alone time at home. I loved
those parts of my life. I loved feeling so independent. I should've
just realized that it would've been way easier to do all those things

if I were to have just been single and not crying over a guy with a questionable hairdo. But you live and learn.

During each of those Manbun breakups, Kristen would try to set me up with Beau. She loves to play matchmaker. Sometimes she gets it wrong, like with me and Jax, but sometimes she gets it right, like with Tom and Katie. Kristen would constantly show me Beau's Instagram and say, "He's just so nice and normal, with a normal job and life. And he's so obsessed with his dog so you'll love him." Normal and nice with a dog—apparently that's all it takes. Even Katie came to me one day and said, "I was at La Piazza at the Grove, and I looked over and saw this guy with some people we knew and he just looked and seemed like someone who would be perfect for you." That person was Beau. I mean, that's pretty bold of her to say that after only just observing him for a little while. They were obviously onto something though.

I was all for a date right away. I thought he was super cute and good-looking on his Instagram. He seemed fun but very different from what I was used to dating, which I thought would be a *good* thing. I mean, let's be honest, Beau has major hipster vibes. He hates it when I say that, but he needs to just learn to embrace the fact that he's a total hipster. I, on the other hand, make fun of hipsters. But I was totally into breaking my pattern and trying to date someone who didn't fit my normal "type," since if my type was Manbun, I needed to change that shit up. I embraced the idea of this hipster dude who is covered in weird tattoos, who wears overalls on the reg, and who probs hangs out at vintage bike shops or something. Just a note: if your relationships have pretty much been toxic, it might be a good move to try to date someone who is completely the opposite of your type, since your type might be an asshole.

Anyway, Beau apparently didn't feel the same way when Kristen would show him my Instagram. Everyone says his reactions were along the lines of: "Um, this blond reality star who probably only goes out if she is getting bottle service at a club? No, thank you." RUDE! I'll never forget, a year into our relationship we were pillow-talking one night and he told me that all jokes aside, it's not that he wasn't into me based on my Instagram but that he thought I would never be interested in someone like him, so why even try? Whether that's lip service or not, I really don't care. It was sweet. Needless to say, throughout all those little Manbun breakups, when my friends were trying to set us up, Beau and I never met. That's on him obviously. I was ready!

It wasn't until a month after my actual final Manbun breakup that I met Beau. I was at home one night seriously enjoying time to myself with my dogs, probably watching *Scream Queens* reruns and drinking sauvignon blanc, when Kristen texted me and said she was having a bunch of people over to watch some fight match with some dude named McGregor. I was like, "Um, no, thank you, that actually sounds like my personal version of hell." She urged me to just buck up and come, since Beau would be there. It was hard to part with *Scream Queens*, but I caved.

For most of the night at Kristen's place, Beau and I didn't even speak. That stupid fight match (that's the technical sports term, right?) kept everyone quiet and glued to the television. Not ideal for flirting. When the match finally ended, I'd had enough, and I decided I wasn't going to wait around for this guy to talk to me, so I marched myself up to him and introduced myself. He remembers me being very chipper and deliberate about it; I remember being fed up with waiting around.

We talked for a while, and I love the fact that Kristen had the wise idea to snap a photo of us meeting for the first time. It's a grainy picture from across the room, and it looks like it was caught by a surveillance camera. Super sketchy. To make it worse, it shows the back of my head, and my extensions look absolutely whack. I won't be framing it, but I love having it. The only thing I remember about our conversation that night was that Beau talked about

Germany and Italy a lot. Like, a lot a lot. I wasn't 100 percent sold on "talks about Europe a lot" guy, but the next day is when we really connected.

Kristen (again) organized a little hangout. We were going to this Alexa Chung party at the Skybar at the Mondrian hotel (I sound like the ultimate basic LA bitch, I know), and Kristen invited Beau to come along. Soon after we each got there, Beau and I huddled on a bench in the corner of the bar and talked all night long. We were the last ones to leave Skybar, and we both just remember laughing the whole night. We realized we lived right down the street from each other, so I told him if this all went horribly wrong, I'd still be able to easily stalk him. I might not have won him over with my filtered Instagram photos, but I lured him in with my winning, sparkling personality. After that night, we did the proper thing, where he took me on a series of dates. The first date was to a tapas restaurant, the second date to Sunday lunch and a movie at the Grove, and on the third date he cooked for me. He made spaghetti Bolognese and tricked me into eating Impossible meat. I'm definitely not a vegetarian, but now we cook with fake meat all the time like total hipsters! Anyway, it was all pretty textbook, but I still appreciated every date. As fun as the dates were, I do remember being super impatient because Beau wasn't making a move. I don't think he even kissed me until we were several dates in, so, since one of my signature traits is impatience, I made the move when it came to our first time sleeping together.

Back before my friends and I moved out of our WeHo apartments, we'd regularly rent these big McMansions for the weekend.

It was so fun to just take over a big house, pretend we lived there, and have a blast all weekend. We did this for Labor Day that year, and when Beau and I arrived separately, Kristen announced that she put both of us in the guesthouse. Neither of us objected—I mean, this was my opportunity to spend the night with him after our series of very PG-rated dates. I thought, *Enough of the gentleman crap!* Beau likes to describe this night as the night I took advantage of him, which is probably fair. The next morning we woke up and cuddled and watched *Chrisley Knows Best* together for hours. We had our dogs in bed with us, and I knew then that I liked him. I mean, how many guys will watch *Chrisley Knows Best* with you and actually enjoy it? Still, I had just gotten out of a traumatic relationship with Manbun, and I was not about to be putting all my eggs in any one basket. I still dated around and did my own thing, as did Beau. I think that mentality is what maybe made me begin to put him in the fuckboy category. That and the fact that he didn't walk me home from his apartment after one date, which I thought was #RudeAF.

After I attacked Beau in the McMansion guesthouse, we averaged about a date a week, but we kept everything very light and easy. Then, in October, Beau went full fuckboy. He didn't ask me out that whole month, but he would watch every single one of my Instagram stories, he would respond and direct message me, and he'd go to all the places where my friends and I hung out—but he never asked to bring me. He "kept in touch," but from a distance. I guess this is called "orbiting." It's standard fuckboy vibes. Then, in late November, out of nowhere, he started asking me out again.

Turns out, he had a full-body rash that he was being tested for. He thought he had scurvy or syphilis or some weird pirate disease that ends up eating your brain. It turned out to be bad eczema outbreaks (which he still gets on the reg), but it gives me a good laugh to this day. I thought he was a fuckboy, when really, he thought he had a disease and didn't want me to see him naked. When he finally did open up to me about all his skin issues, it wound up being something we bonded over because I am the psoriasis and rosacea queen. He felt more comfortable being shirtless around me, and I ended up feeling more comfortable going without makeup. I had spent our first dating months never letting him see me sans makeup. I'd sleep in that shit and just secretly touch it up when I woke up. So when he told me about his rash, it was comforting knowing he had the same type of insecurities.

Since I was coming out of a horrific relationship, I had a lot of hesitation when it came to getting into a new one, so I kept treating Beau as a fling, but a fling with promise. I guess I kind of tricked him into thinking I was a totally independent woman and the opposite of needy. Joke is on him now, because I'm clingy AF. Basically, I played the dating game perfectly without even realizing that I was doing it. I had unknowingly become that chill "cool girl"—cue the Tove Lo song. I just wasn't taking anything seriously, and when I felt he was acting fuckboy-like, I never confronted him about it. I never had a drunken freak-out where I texted him a million times. (I saved that for when I locked him in.) I never showed up where he was, like a stalker. I never got bitchy if I ran into him at a bar, asking him why he hadn't invited me. I was just really enjoying my single life. Nothing he did or didn't do could truly get to me, because I had only put maybe one or two eggs in the Beau basket, instead of the full twelve. So I guess he thought I was hard to get, which, like I said, joke's on him.

I remember the exact moment I realized Beau was actually someone I could truly be with long term, and that moment ironically fits in with this book. The very first time I got canceled, after I had done a podcast episode on my #MeToo movement thoughts, was truly a dark time. I had lost almost all my sponsors, and it was the first time I had to really start over with my podcast. Beau was constantly messaging and calling me about it. He was so reassuring, so uplifting. One day, he walked over to my apartment and gave me a present. It was the book *Good Night Stories for Rebel Girls*, which is a children's book that tells stories of one hundred awesome women, from Elizabeth I to Malala. He had written me a note inside the book that read, "To Stassi: Be a motherfucking sparkly ass butterfly." He explained that I should look at the situation as if I were a caterpillar and that I was going to emerge from this major setback as a sparkly butterfly. We stayed up until four in the morning, and he made me sing girl-power songs like the Chicks' "Not Ready to Make Nice." It was so truly kind, and it made me feel so strong. I realized that Beau was the exact type of man I wanted to end up with—someone who wanted to empower me. I had never had that before. And that's when I really started falling for him. I mean, how could I not?

When we did start to get serious, I had to figure out how to handle the whole *I'm on reality TV so therefore our relationship might be on TV too* thing. Some people have to have a conversation about the fact that they work long hours at their law firm, and I knew I was going to have to talk to Beau about maybe being on *Vanderpump*. I had to maneuver through those conversations very delicately. I remember sitting at a sushi restaurant in West Hollywood with him one night, and I figured since the sake was flowing, it might be a great time to bring up the idea of him doing the show. Boy was I shut down. He gave me a very firm "No way in hell."

I'll never forget the way I felt when my heart sank into my booty and my blood ran cold. Was this going to be another Man-bun situation? I couldn't bear another relationship like that. Man-bun made my life so hard all the time because he hated the show, so when we broke up, I promised myself I would never put myself in that position again. The show was my job; my core group of friends were on it with me. I wanted to date someone who would be willing to go with the flow and do the show with me, even if it was a few tiny scenes. Beau explained that it just wasn't his thing and he didn't want it to affect his career. He worked in casting, but he was also a commercial actor, and he worked nonstop doing commercials. The second you do reality TV, a career as a commercial actor just isn't realistic anymore. There is such a stigma around anyone in the reality world, and you become somewhat of an "influencer," for lack of a better term. It's hard to be the dad in a Tide commercial when people might go, "Um, that's Beau from *Vanderpump*—when did he get a six-year-old son?"

I understood everything he was saying, but *my* career required me to share every aspect of my life. I can't share everything and then not share the most important thing, which is my relationship. I resolved to keep calm, finish my sake, come up with a plan, and wait until Beau was a little more in love with me to bring it up again. Super sneaky. The first part of my plan involved me introducing him to everyone in the show. He was already getting to know all my friends, and he was slowly becoming a part of the "group." That helped my cause because he began to genuinely love everyone and consider them his own best friends. When I introduced him to our producers, and once he started becoming close to them, my plan was almost complete!

Beau loved my friends, and he loved my producers, but then he started to see that everything we would be filming would be things he would end up feeling FOMOish about, like parties, nights out at bars, Sunday-funday brunch, vacations. I may condemn him for it all the time, but thank *God* for Beau's FOMO. He didn't want to miss out on these times where he could hang out with all his friends. So then a few months later, when I felt the time was right, I brought up the prospect of him doing the show again—and he agreed. I was elated. On cloud nine. It was the opposite of rock bottom. And what's even better is that he actually ended up loving doing the show, which doesn't always happen. He became somewhat of an MVP of *Vanderpump* at times. Our producers loved him because he was so laid-back and easy to work with, and he brought this "normal quirky guy" energy that our group needed. He always somehow manages to make things lighter, and I think people really appreciate that about him. He helped me out too because he made me seem likable. Honest to God, I owe that to him. He balanced out my bitchiness, he softened me, and I matured more with him as my partner. He brings out the best in me, and that really helped me navigate *Vanderpump Rules* and become a much better version of season-one Stassi.

And now we're married with a kid! I feel like I have a small right to brag about my relationship since I endured so many awful ones for so many years *and* it all happened on television for the world to judge. Why is it that we're often afraid to talk about how great our relationships are? Are we scared of seeming braggy? Are we scared of being annoying? I feel like most people bond over complaining about their relationships, but not gonna lie, I don't often really have anything to contribute to those types of conversations, and I find myself holding back from talking at all because for the most part I only have good things to say about my life with Beau. I wish we could change that mentality and make it okay to brag sometimes without sounding like an asshole.

Here, I'll show you: Hi, my name is Stassi, and I love the shit out of my relationship.

Now that that's out of the way, of course every relationship still has kinks that need to be worked out. Not everything is easy AF all the time, especially when there is a worldwide pandemic or when one of you is being canceled, or both at the same time. Of course there have also been little things we've had to work on pre-pandemic and pre-canceling. There was a time when it really bothered me how much Beau loved to stay up and socialize. I hesitate to call it "partying" because he isn't out at the clubs or anything, but Beau loves a good Sunday funday or a good night out at his favorite bar, and he loves to stay up late with friends. At first, this seemed ideal because he so easily blended in with my group of friends, and the fact that I can take him anywhere makes my life so much easier. But I'm someone who tires quickly. I love to socialize for like two hours, and then I'm done. This was something I really had to get used to, especially since I'm of the mind that nothing good ever happens after midnight. You could say I'm a little scarred by my ex-boyfriends' and friends' past indiscretions. It seemed that any time someone was shady or unfaithful, it always happened after hours. It took me quite a long time to break that mentality and not let the mistakes of my exes affect how I deal with Beau, and luckily for me he was very patient with that.

After season seven aired and I freaked out on Beau twice on national television because he wanted to stay out late (once on my birthday and once in Mexico), we both decided we should go to couples therapy to discuss it. He had never given me any reason not to trust him, so why was I constantly freaking out if he wanted to stay out late? After about three therapy sessions, I realized it was all because of my past experiences, and we came up with ways to help us deal with my fear of being betrayed by someone again. It helped Beau to hear me talk about my fears and worries and about what I had gone through that led me to have those fears. He wasn't angry that I freaked out on him after that, and he understood it and could work with it. So in order to help, we agreed that before we went out, if he wanted to stay out late, he would tell me ahead of time, and I'd be prepared for it. That actually made a huge difference, as opposed to me drunkenly freaking out on him at one in the morning if he wasn't tired yet. I guess it always helped that I was always invited or welcome to stay out with him as well. It's not like he was being sneaky. I began to shift my focus. When he stayed out late, I got to be home by myself, like the days when I was single. Once I started looking at it as something I enjoy, it became a win-win situation for him to stay out without me. Nowadays, I'd kill for "me time." We do take Hartford out to the Belmont or to brunch, and she's a very cheap and adorable AF date. In that way I guess being a mom agrees with me, because when I say I'm ready to go home and get in bed at 8:00 p.m., no one can argue because I'm a freaking mom.

I've always felt that Beau and I are stronger together than we are separate. Before Covid and the Canceling, I had decided to commit myself to touring and being on the road for a while, so we had to talk about what that meant for our relationship. I'd be out of town most of the year, so would Beau stay in LA and work in casting? He already couldn't go on commercial auditions anymore, because *Vanderpump Rules* had made him too recognizable. So we had to come up with a plan. I decided to point-blank ask him if he would be okay shifting his life in support of me. What if we both worked on my career together? I've always seen myself being in a marriage where I wore the pants and was the breadwinner. I love working, and I love providing. All I've wanted in a partner was love, respect, support, and joy. Beau brings all of that and more, so why not go on tour with me? He makes my job easier, he makes me more entertaining, I love performing with him, and so I thought, let's be a duo. At first he was hesitant, I think because working in casting was his last piece of manly independence. But we worked well together, and traveling and touring together seemed like a once-in-a-lifetime opportunity, so he agreed to it. We had it figured out. Yes, he could do casting when he was in town, but for the most part, he toured and performed with me, and he did *Vanderpump Rules* with me. I don't know how and if I would've been able to tour without him.

When Covid struck and the tour was rescheduled, we took a major hit. Beau had given up his job to work with me, so now what? Because of the pandemic, there weren't exactly a lot of casting sessions happening. Then when I got canceled, shit really hit the fan. Because Beau was associated with me, no one wanted to work with him. That was devastating to deal with. I can handle being fired, I can handle being ridiculed and tossed aside (sort of), but to toss aside my partner for *my* mistakes is something that shook me to my very core. The amount of guilt I still carry around tears me to shreds. It wasn't just me who was hurt financially because of the firing, now it was my other half. I watched his coworkers unfollow him on social media; I watched all his contracts fall through and his brand partnerships get canceled. That's truly what I hate the most about cancel culture—the loved ones or friends or kids it affects. During that time there was a good month where I felt like Beau shut down. We never fought, but I felt distant. We were in the same house, sleeping in the same bed, but he wasn't himself. He was down, he was closed off, and it wasn't until a few weeks of me begging him to talk to me about it that he was willing to open up.

When he did, we sat and cried together and talked about how scared we were, and then we brainstormed plans. No, we weren't losing our house or anything (yet), but it's scary when you're used to making a certain income and that's taken away. It's scary when you're a couple who works together, because when one of you gets canceled, that means the other one does too, by default. The second we acknowledged this and said it all out loud, it was like a huge weight was lifted for him. We were close again, he was happier again, he laughed again. Open communication for the win, amirite?! The first lesson I learned when it comes to having a healthy marriage is to always talk through everything together. And I mean everything. I'm thankful I'm married to a man who was raised by a single mother who is also a therapist, because communication is like second nature to him.

So let's set aside the fact that I married a hipster (much more on this later), and not just that—a hipster who doesn't know he's a hipster. Because besides that, I think Beau is everything my little fifteen-year-old heart desired, even if I wasn't thinking about marriage 24-7. If you read *Next Level Basic*, you know I was madly in love with Ewan McGregor's character in *Moulin Rouge!* I loved the love he had with Nicole Kidman's character. It sounds cheesy, but they were just so obsessed with each other! And now I have that type of love. I just didn't expect him to be wearing overalls.

Rock-Bottom TAKEAWAY

Basically, if your relationships have all been disasters and you meet someone who does not seem like your type *at all*, that might mean you're destined to fall in love. Beau has been by my side through some seriously rock-bottom times, and he's listened and brought me ice cream Snickers bars and helped me get through tough times by singing power ballads with me. If you're scared that someone is just a fuckboy/-girl but you also feel like there might be more there, give it a chance, because it might just turn out that they were (temporarily) ghosting you because of a full-body skin rash or an embarrassing bout of adult acne or something. In sum, in matters of the heart, be open-minded and make the first move if you must. It might just turn out okay.

Stassi's Recs for Marrying Your Fuckboy

Become a "cool girl": Listen carefully, because you can't *pretend* to be the cool girl, you have to *become* one. The problem with pretending to be the cool girl is that you end up playing games because you feel like you have to act in ways that aren't really true to how you feel, and playing games is exhausting, frustrating, and, IMO, dishonest. I've never benefited from playing games while dating. I feel like you can totally see through it, and it looks even more desperate than if you were to just be honest and vulnerable. On top of that, playing games always made me feel irritable because I just wasn't being myself. So pretending to be all chill really doesn't help anyone in the situation, and at some point, you're most likely going to explode, show up at his/her house unexpectedly, and just drunkenly undo all the hard, exhausting work you put in anyway. This is why you must *become* the cool girl. Here are some steps you can take:

✻ **Don't put all your eggs in one basket:** You guys aren't official yet, so why bank on this one person? Stay on your dating app, and stay open to new people. There is nothing wrong with dating around if you're honest about it. I've made the mistake of deleting my dating app the second I went on one good first date because I thought that first date meant we were destined to be together forever. Boy was I wrong. Please, learn from my mistakes. It takes a while to get to know someone, so until you're sure of this person, stay open to new people and experiences.

✳ **Say yes to everything:** I think 2016 was my self-proclaimed "year of yes" (I see you, Shonda Rhimes). I just said yes to everything. Well, almost everything. I wasn't engaging in threesomes or going on ayahuasca retreats or anything like that. If a friend invited me to a party, I said yes. A vacation that didn't involve ayahuasca, yep. A new job, yep. A date, yep. My best friends' honeymoon? Said yes to that too. I actually flew to Bora Bora alone to meet my friends Katie and Tom in the middle of their honeymoon. Yes, I was invited. I love being a homebody, but I realized that I was never going to meet new people or really evolve if I was just sitting at home watching *Gossip Girl* reruns night after night. As fun as that may be, it doesn't really get you anywhere. You're not going to meet the love of your life, or your new best friends, or get that new job opportunity by staying home. Totally get that that's hard to do during a pandemic, and I wish I had advice for you then, but I definitely do not. If you're not in a pandemic, and if you're saying yes to everything, then that leaves no time to sit at home and stalk that dude's Instagram stories, because you're out being busy and being a cool girl and doing your own thing.

✳ **Find the things that you like about being single:** I'm pretty sure this is why Beau thought I was such a "cool girl." I actually enjoyed being single and being by myself. Of course I wanted to find a true-love relationship, but because I liked being alone so much, I wasn't obsessed with getting there right away. What is it about being single that you like? Do you love being able to go to happy hour after work without having to report to someone? Do you love sleeping in a bed alone? Do you like eating a whole box of mac 'n' cheese without someone being there to judge you? I personally found that I loved taking girl trips, I loved going to brunches with my friends, and I loved my nights at home by myself. Yes, I could technically do some of those things when Beau and I got serious, but not in the same way. A girls' trip now is like a once-a-year thing (at most). A girls' brunch now needs to be planned a week in advance (or more, once you have kids). Life isn't as carefree as it was when I was single—not even close. So enjoy it while you can.

✳ **Instagram yourself happy:** Roll your eyes all you want, but this is simple and effective. People want to be around happy people and date happy people (for the most part—I guess some people love a grouch). Use your social media to showcase yourself doing things you like. People will gravitate toward you because you look confident and assured, like you don't need a man or woman to make you happy. For me, I posted Instagram Stories when I was on trips, when I was working on things I loved, or when I was just feeling happy. If Beau would've seen all those embarrassing crying videos I posted when I was going through my breakup with Manbun, he totally would've had a different opinion of me. No one wants to be around mopey people. Yes, we all feel down or depressed sometimes, but if you're trying to attract someone, do everything you can to refrain from posting cryptic quotes and "I'm depressed" videos. You need to ease people into that part of your life. This may seem harsh, but I have been the girl posting weird drunken "I'm sad," videos and it never got me anywhere. So what are the things that make you happiest? Do you love horses? Post yourself riding horses. Do you love nature? (Gross, BTW.) Post pics of yourself hiking or paddleboarding or whatever nature people do. Just find where you glow and let it shine, on Instagram, with filters. Give people FOMO that they're not hanging out with *you*.

✳ **Refrain from sending psycho texts until your crush has said "I love you"**: This may seem like game playing, but I just look at it as "postponing the inevitable." No one has ever gotten anywhere by sending a slew of psycho, clingy texts. We've all done it, but has it ever worked to your advantage? It has never freaking worked. It may feel good for those thirteen seconds it takes to type out, but once you press Send, you're left panicking and wishing you could crawl into the screen and take it back. So you just sit and wait for that text bubble to come up . . . and sometimes that waiting can go on for days. Psycho texts are no fun for anyone, so do yourself a favor and wait to show your person this side of you, because we all have this side to us. Wait until you're well into your relationship, when he/she loves you so much that there is no turning back. That's what I did. If I ever got irritated with Beau,

I just digested it and went about my day and found something to do that made me happy. I probably went to Neiman Marcus, got drunk off espresso martinis, and bought a pair of Chanel ballet flats or something. I waited until at least six months after he said he loved me to send him seventy-nine psycho texts in a row. One of my first early memories of finally showing my psycho side to Beau was embarrassingly caught on camera for *Vanderpump Rules* at my winter-themed thirtieth birthday party. Beau wouldn't come to bed with me, and he wanted to stay out with our friends, so I had a major meltdown. I broke my own phone and lost my mind. Those were the days. By that time, he was already too invested and too in love with me, so there was no way a measly seventy-nine psycho texts were going to make him break up with me. [Insert evil genius laugh.]

✳ **Show him/her that life with you is fun:** This kind of goes along with my previous advice, but no one wants to commit themselves to a life without fun. I mean, do you?! A lot of women just wait around for their boyfriend/girlfriend to take the lead and plan things, but I think there is so much power in being the planner. Yes, there should be a balance and it shouldn't always fall on you, but taking initiative is beneficial in a relationship. Plan date nights, plan trips, dream up fun activities, wake up one Sunday and say, "Fuck it, let's put our Sunday chores aside and barhop all day." God, I miss those days. I personally want to have fun and laugh my way through life, and seeing that Beau was such a positive, happy, fun person was a major reason I wanted to spend my life with him. So show your partner that life with you will always be fun—that is, unless you hate fun. I feel like that's how I truly locked him in, and how he locked me in too.

If all else fails, use witchcraft: Maybe I'm kidding—but maybe I'm not! I mean, could casting a love spell *hurt*? I personally don't see any downside to this. If the spell doesn't work, what's the worst that could happen? You got drunk with your girlfriends and wasted $25 on candles and herbs for a love potion? At this point you have nothing to lose, and at least you'll have a funny story to tell. I say, cast away.

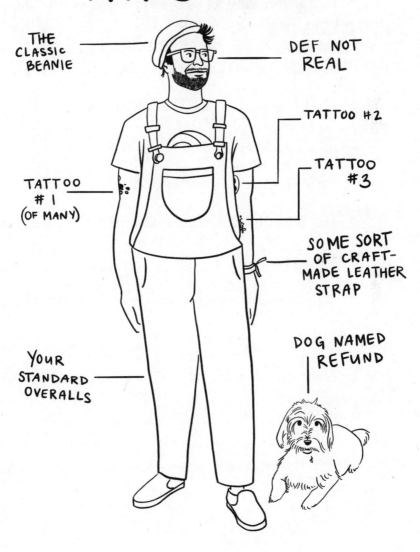

ANATOMY OF A HIPSTER

THE CLASSIC BEANIE

DEF NOT REAL

TATTOO #2

TATTOO #3

TATTOO #1 (OF MANY)

SOME SORT OF CRAFT-MADE LEATHER STRAP

DOG NAMED REFUND

YOUR STANDARD OVERALLS

✳ He wears overalls.

✳ He actually made a motorized bicycle.

✳ He has a tattoo for all the favorite places he's traveled (among 2,837,462,389 more tattoos).

✳ He'd give anything for me to allow him to sport a mustache.

✳ He makes his own bespoke limoncino.

✳ He's had almost everything pierced, ear gauges included.

✳ He owns fake eyeglasses.

✳ He loves a handmade leather good.

✳ He's definitely not afraid of a flea market.

✳ Loves a beanie.

✳ Went through a musical theater phase . . . as an adult.

✳ Paints his own wall art.

✳ Named his dog Refund, which, to me, is a hipster move.

CHAPTER 6

Not-So-Social Media

We live in a time where branding is everything, so one thing can go wrong on social and everything comes crashing down on you, career-wise.

> Is the above quote from:
> A. Meghan Markle
> B. Megan Thee Stallion
> C. *Emily in Paris*
> D. His Holiness the Dalai Lama
> E. Stassi Schroeder Clark

The correct answer is E, me, writing in my book *Next Level Basic* and having no clue that a few years later everything *would* come crashing down via social media in a million hateful Instagram comments and tweets and Facebook posts. Back then, I wrote a chapter called "How to Look Hot on Social," and now it's more like, "How to Survive on Social and Not Lose Every Shred of Confidence You've Ever Had." Let me tell you, it's much more fun when your only worry is looking glowy and mastering a pose that hides your double chin. Sometimes I miss those carefree days.

After the Canceling, social media became a no-fly zone for me for a while. I imagine downfalls before social media were a little easier to handle, because what were haters going to do? Hire a skywriting plane to draw "I Hate You #Loser" in the air above your house? Skywriting dissolves in like ten minutes, but tweets are forever. I guess being forced to wear a scarlet letter around town was embarrassing, so now evil Instagram comments are like our modern scarlet letter. It's not just embarrassing though. It's horrible, it's a psychological nightmare, and it can affect anyone, whether you have twenty followers or two million. Honestly, if you get five thousand positive comments and one evil comment, all you'll think about for the rest of your life is the one evil comment. It'll haunt you forever, unless you train yourself to not read the comments, which is pretty much impossible. Who has that much willpower?! Everyone reads the comments. Even the strongest humans have their masochistic doom-scrolling moments of weakness. Chrissy Teigen does it. She even quit Twitter because of the trolls! So, it happens.

For a while there, social media officially became the virtual Hunger Games for me. Before I even got canceled, the early months of Covid and quarantine made social media the most depressing thing ever. FOMO was D-E-A-D. Everyone went on Instagram preaching that we should use the time stuck at home to learn a hobby or write that book you've always thought about writing, maybe learn a language, or master baking or knitting. I would scroll through and think, *Calm the eff down, everyone!* While all those overachievers were advising me to use my time wisely by making banana bread and becoming a kundalini yoga expert, I was rocking back and forth in the fetal position after having binged *Real Housewives of New York City* for the third time, just trying to not have a total mental/emotional breakdown.

What's worse is that since we were all stuck at home with nothing to do, I checked social media even more. I think I was clocking over six hours of screen time a day. It became a vicious cycle I couldn't stop. I knew social media was making me feel semi-depressed, yet I had nothing to do *but* check social media. It was so not ideal. Then once I got canceled, social media became the Hunger Games stuck inside the Upside Down from *Stranger Things*. It felt like every other thing on my home feed was about me, and not in a fun *It's my birthday so everyone is posting about me* type way. Every comment and DM was about how awful people thought I was and how I deserved to be officially done, banished, shamed. So on top of feeling like an underachiever who had yet to learn French, I was also being told that I should just disappear. That's why, for me, I stopped caring about how to look hot on social and started thinking about whether I should delete all my accounts and move into a cave in Romania.

One of the most frustrating parts of the Canceling was being unable to connect with people. I made a choice to go silent, since everything I said or did was being magnified and taken out of context, and it was better for my mental health to step away for a while. There was a Facebook group that some of my Khaleesis made called "Straight Up with Stassi: Khaleesis." It's a group page unlike any I've ever seen because every member is supportive and kind to one another and not trying to tear each other apart. I've never seen any Facebook bullying on this page. It never gets cruel and out of hand, thanks to the people who are monitoring it. I've always felt like it was a safe place for me to go and connect with my Khaleesis.

For months after I was canceled, I so desperately wanted to post something on that page. I wanted to thank them for being open to the idea that I could learn and be better. Some of the members sent me pregnancy gifts, and I was truly touched. But every time I went to go write something, I had to remind myself that I couldn't. What if someone had joined that group just to screenshot things and blast them on Page Six or wherever? That group, which was once safe, felt unsafe. I mean, people did find my home address (you can google anything, I guess), which freaked Beau's mom out so much she started to have dreams that I was going to be the next

Sharon Tate, murdered in my own home by a 2020 Charles Manson. As much as I love murder houses, I don't want to actually be murdered in my house, so her dreams freaked me out.

The greatest thing about social media is that it's an incredible tool for connecting to other people, yet during such a difficult time, when I wanted to connect the most, I couldn't use it for that very reason. I would check the Facebook page often, and I felt so gutted when I would read something like, "I wish Stassi would at least say something here . . . If she really cared she'd say something here." I wanted to scream, "I do care! I care so much!" But I just couldn't risk making things worse for myself. Sorry, Khaleesis!

Staying quiet and off social media was an active choice I made for myself. My crisis publicist (I don't think it'll ever *not* feel weird to say that) wanted me to get out there and keep posting things about my life, but it just didn't feel right to me. Not only was it just not my time to shine or attract attention, but I was also scared and didn't want to deal with all the negative comments, especially being that I was newly pregnant. When you get canceled or fired, everyone has a different opinion about how they think you should handle it and what they think you should do next. I kept having to remind everyone that it's easy to dish out advice when you're not the one at rock bottom. I've always been pretty good at trusting my instincts, but during this time I really mastered it. My instincts were telling me to go dark for a while, to stay off social media, to focus on my health and pregnancy, and to quietly start my journey of growth. The only post I wanted to share was my gender-reveal post, because after my pregnancy was leaked, I was not about to let that be taken from me too. So I stayed quiet through all the *You're gonna have a racist baby* comments, because announcing the baby's gender was so important to me. A lot of people saw this post and thought it meant that I didn't care about what had happened, that I was entirely unremorseful, or that I was trying to take attention away from the cancellation with my pregnancy. All that was a little tough to swallow, but at the end of the day, I was happy I got to announce my baby girl to the world myself.

Eventually I crept back to social media, and I would occasionally post something about my pregnancy on my Instagram Stories since that way I didn't have to see mean comments. Because my pregnancy had become public, and I wasn't going to get to go the Kylie Jenner–recluse route, I still wanted to share little bits of the experience with my friends, family, and the followers who still cared. I wanted to be in charge of my pregnancy narrative, not the paparazzi. I refused to let the only glimpses of my pregnancy be through the lens of "the paps" and tabloids. While I was happy to share little pieces of my pregnancy journey here and there, it didn't feel completely right that I hadn't spoken out about what happened yet. But like I said earlier, I wanted to wait until I felt like I had digested everything and had something meaningful to say. I couldn't and wouldn't rush it. I waited to really rejoin social media until after I spoke out. And let me tell you, that first post back was *terrifying*. I posted about being twenty-five weeks pregnant, and I was shocked by all the support I received. I had fully prepared myself for the worst. Isn't it crazy how something as simple as posting a photo can cause so much anxiety and self-doubt? It doesn't matter how many followers you have or who you are—there are always people out there on social media who can affect how we feel about ourselves, which can be dangerous if we're not careful. I'm not going to quit social media completely because I am a basic bitch at heart and I love it, but I have learned to protect myself a little bit. I'm only human though, so not reading the comments is hard AF.

I've said this before, but I think one of the keys to being successful on social media is to not be too curated. My Instagram page isn't particularly aesthetically pleasing. There's no color scheme or theme. I pretty much just post what I feel at that moment. It has been a very new experience for me to have to start overthinking things. Now I overthink every photo, every caption, every comment I leave. Not only am I scared of offending someone, but I'm also under a microscope. People are looking for me to mess up again, wanting me to screw up so they can point and say, "See, I told you she sucked!" At one point, I was even worried that people might look at the fact that I was pinning cake recipes on Pinterest and take that to mean that I was an evil baker who wasn't taking my canceling seriously.

I braved Instagram, but I didn't dare venture into the Twitter world so fast. Instagram has been a little easier because it's a space for you to share your life, not only with your followers, but with your friends. Twitter is a space to share opinions and thoughts with . . . anyone and everyone. Unless you make your account private, but what's the point of that? Why tweet into a void? For a long time I was in no position to be sharing opinions or thoughts.

If Instagram is the Hunger Games in the Upside Down, then Twitter is the Hunger Games in the Upside Down swallowed by *The Conjuring* universe and then beaten over the head by Jigsaw or Leatherface. I am petrified of Twitter.

So maybe I'm scared to tweet, but, embarrassing as this might be—I got into TikTok! What a glorious safe space it is! It's so innocent! It's filled with dancing families, people giving helpful advice, cooking hacks, or just random funny or interesting videos. I can't believe I rejected it for so long. I can't even begin to explain how many baby-tips videos I saved. I actually signed up for an account, and it took me forever to finally post something. My first post showed Hartford (of course) as a sweet baby during the day but an evil baby at night on her monitor (it was funny, I swear). It's another outlet where I don't feel so vulnerable, and I'm all about it.

Another corner of social media that opened up to me was that I experienced "message boards" for the first time in my life! The moment I found out I was pregnant, I downloaded the What to Expect app, just like every other pregnant woman in history. I bet Neanderthal mamas had a What to Expect cave-painting message board. In this app, they put you in a group based on your due date. I was placed in the January 2021 group. Every day I received an email that said "Daily Digest for the January 2021 Babies Group," which was a daily update on our group's message board discussions. Let me tell you, opening up that email was the highlight of my day for nine months. Every day around 4:45 p.m., I'd start refreshing my email to see if it had come, and I'd stop whatever I was doing to go through those message boards. I loved that I had this whole community of women who were experiencing the same things I was. I never actually joined in and contributed anything, but I will say there were times I was tempted to be like, "Hello, Stassi Schroeder here, anyone else experiencing extreme constipation?!" I managed to refrain.

Eventually the sweet message boards reared their ugly head. It was crazy to see that, like Instagram, Facebook, and Twitter, this pregnancy community app also was a place filled with trolling and judgment. This was my first introduction to mom-shaming. Whenever I saw a thread title like *Occasional glass of wine, no judgment please* or *Why I stopped my prenatals*, I knew it was time to pop some popcorn and sit back and enjoy the show, because I was about to witness mommy catfights galore. The amount of mom-shaming was *shocking*. As much as I didn't like seeing other people get attacked over their choices, it made me realize again that I wasn't the only one being attacked on social media. It's not just fired reality stars who get pummeled online, it's everyone. And I have to admit there was a twisted kind of comfort I got in that, knowing that it wasn't just me. Mom boards are not for the weak.

Taking a long social media break to focus on my life (and to creep on TikTok and mom boards) was actually kind of refreshing. You know when you're playing video games and you've been trying to beat a level, and when you finally do, you just want to take a major weeklong break where you can just bask in the fact that your character is safe, before you start trying for the next level? That's what taking a break from social felt like. I was safe, and still alive, just resting in between video game levels. Yes, I just made a video game analogy because sometimes I play a little *Mario Bros.* or *Crash Bandicoot* to soothe the soul. I'm not a gamer by any means, but I dabble.

Anyway, I had just gotten through being canceled (which was one level), and I knew when I rejoined social media again, it would be like starting the next level. I actually very much enjoyed my break from social media. There were definitely times I felt left out, as well as times where nice things happened and I felt sad that I couldn't share them. But for the most part, it felt like a huge weight was lifted. That feeling I had right when Covid started, when I felt like I wasn't doing enough with my time? That feeling went away. I had nothing to prove anymore. I didn't have to worry about churning out content. I didn't compare myself to anyone anymore because what did it matter? All the pressure was off. I didn't have to look my best, I didn't have to win at pregnancy life, I didn't have to be "on." I could just chill and really be present. That might even be why I had such an easy pregnancy, since I was so relaxed. (Minus the stress of watching my career crumble before my eyes.)

I like to think I'm pretty good at not letting trolls get to me now. I never really engage, but if things get toxic, I do occasionally block people. Beau is not great at handling trolls. I had to talk him off the ledge quite a few times over the summer of 2020. There were so many times he wanted to write back, and I had to do everything short of stapling his hands to the chair to prevent him from doing it. Nothing good ever comes from fighting back on social media. Think about it. It's like arguing with a three-year-old who has no idea what they're talking about. Strangers like to have an opinion even when they know nothing about the reality of a situation. I remind myself of that every time I am annoyed.

People read a click-bait headline on some trashy pop culture news website and think they have the whole story—they think they know who you are to your very core. It's ridiculous. And what trolls want is attention, which is something I absolutely refuse to give them. Why would I ever give the bad guys what they want? That's why you'll never see me fight back. However, there is one exception. When I've just hit my limit, or when I see someone has written something truly gross and mean, instead of hitting back, I just comment something like "You're fun," which highlights their original post for everyone to see.

Another pro tip is to try to imagine what your troll must be like in real life. Like what must a person be going through for them to viciously attack someone they don't know online? I've never once had the urge to attack someone via social, have you? Those people can't possibly be happy. They can't be living their best lives. I know Beyoncé isn't online trying to cancel people, and everyone should aspire to be like Beyoncé. I'm not saying have empathy for your trolls and invite them to dinner, but maybe remember that they're probably not actually all that happy, and that should help you ignore the hate.

Does it seem like online fighting is worse than ever, or am I just new to this internet subculture shit?! Is it because we were all stuck at home so long—scared, quarantined, and sometimes jobless, so we figured, what the hell?! We can't get our anger out at our kick-boxing classes anymore, so let's head to Twitter! I mean, that's truly what it felt like. Who are these people who just sit at home and rip people to shreds? Like, where do they hide? Where do they hang out? Do they walk among us? Do we go to the same restaurants? Have I walked by someone who took pleasure in trying to ruin my life? It's kind of chilling.

I have to admit, as scary as social media got for me, I missed OOTDs so freaking much during my absence. When I found out I was pregnant, the first thing I did was make a "pregnancy looks" mood board on Pinterest. I was so excited to develop my pregnancy style. I wanted to look Parisian chic and classic. Basically I just wanted to look like a pregnant French woman. But guess what? That never happened. I started buying all these outfits that I thought would look great, and I never wore any of them. First, where did I have to go? And second, I wasn't really prepared to deal with the lack of control surrounding my body. The weight gain in places I had never experienced was hard for me to handle. I wish I was one of those pregnant women who just fully embraced their new body as something beautiful and magical because it's housing a baby. I wasn't that person. I had quite a few meltdowns in my closet. I just missed being able to walk without my thighs chafing. Is that so much to ask?! Is it so hard to look like Hilaria Baldwin and Emily Ratajkowski days after childbirth? Yes. Yes it is.

Because of my insecurities (and, let's face it, my ever-expanding ass), it was challenging to put together any sort of chic OOTDs. After one of my pregnant paparazzi photos came out, I came across a series of comments about how people thought I would have had better maternity OOTDs. Talk about a dagger to the heart! After going through pregnancy, I am a firm believer that we need to go easy on pregnant women regarding their style. It doesn't matter if you're a supermodel, every pregnant woman is struggling with her ever-changing body. Oftentimes I wonder what I would've done had we been filming my pregnancy on *Vanderpump*. I mean, maybe the silver lining of being fired was that I was able to just chill in my loungewear at home 24-7.

I think I took maybe three maternity OOTDs the whole time I was pregnant, and photos of me in sweats and heels do not count. At night I would sometimes dream about what it would be like to have life back to normal, with places to wear cute outfits to, and a body that fit all my stylish clothes. Then I would wake up and put on sweatpants again. I will say I acquired a pretty decent collection of maternity cashmere loungewear, but it was nothing to write home about. I longed for that OOTD life to come back. To make myself feel better about missing my own OOTD life, I bought my daughter a Harry Potter Mirror of Erised mini OOTD mirror for her nursery. I would just live vicariously through her!

The first few weeks, I felt so protective of our baby. She was our whole life though, so it felt awkward not to share that. It was definitely scary sharing that first post with Hartford, because if anyone had said anything even slightly mean about her I would have died of grief. When she was first born, I felt an intense need for privacy, so we kept her to ourselves, which just gave the paparazzi more of a reason to camp out to get that first photo. I wanted them to leave, and I knew that if I posted a photo of her they'd probably scamper away. Their shot wouldn't be worth anything, so there'd be no reason for them to stay. I wanted to control how she got out in the world. Once I posted that first photo, it became so much fun. I mean, she's so freaking cute! Even though there was one troll who said that Hartford looked like the cartoon character Elmer Fudd. I mean, she's gorg, but what two-week-old baby *doesn't* look like Elmer Fudd? The artist who drew him was probably looking at a newborn. Some people also tried to shame me by saying I put an Instagram filter on my baby. Um, of course there was a filter because *my* old-ass face was in the photo. What do people expect?

Should I be ashamed of myself for being excited about baby OOTDs? I read about all these moms, especially in Hollywood, who are supes protective of their children and keep them off social at all costs, but I don't feel that way. I love posting photos and videos of her. Posting photos also helped me realize that her personal style is not girly. Bows look cute in her hair, but she's a minimalist, and she really shines when her outfits are simple, chic, and timeless. That's definitely her vibe.

Maybe it's because my whole adult life was exposed online and on TV and in tabloids that I forgot what true privacy is. I'm so used to sharing my life on television, on my podcast, and on social media that it doesn't even register that I'd be allowed to keep her hidden. I'm sure I'll get a lot of heat for posting my baby constantly, but I think this is just the world we live in. Social media is a huge part of our culture, sharing is a huge part of our culture, and I love sharing the greatest thing in my life—my baby. Maybe ask me this again when she's a preteen. I might feel differently and try to hide her in a cave somewhere. For now, I'm all about it. I do consider every post with Hartford's best interest in mind. Right now it's cute to post cute outfits or milestones or blowouts, but as she gets older, she'll probably have an opinion about what we share. Highly doubt Instagram will even be a thing by then, but you never know.

Rock-Bottom TAKEAWAY

Social media can be the best thing in a basic bitch's life, and it can also be the freaking worst. It does not matter how many followers you have—that one evil troll who says your baby looks like Elmer Fudd or who hashtags #loser in the comments of your post will haunt you forever if you let them. The trick is not to let them. So while I had tons of advice about looking hot on social, my advice about staying safe and sane on social is this: it's scary out there, so watch your back (but not your comments)! That's it. That's the advice. We have all gotten so mean because of social media. I mean, have you *been* on Twitter? It's crazy out there. But it can also be fun, it can be a way to connect, and it can be the perfect place to show off your baby's fashion sense with an adorbs OOTD. So, have fun, do you, and try to shake off the haters as much as you can. They are *not* worth it. If you're feeling super annoyed, you can always reply with something like "You seem nice," and then leave it at that. It doesn't really work to go into attack mode online, so if all else fails, block them!

How to Look Hot on Social While Pregnant

I know I've spent most of this chapter talking about how scary and dark and evil social media can be, but as a true basic bitch, of course I still love it (I just don't love the trolls). Because most of us don't look like Hilaria Baldwin and Emily Ratajkowski, here are some tips that might help you look, if not *hot*, then at least halfway decent on social when you're with child.

Don't get lazy: Wake up, shower, and do your hair and makeup every day, or *almost* every day. This was the only thing that kept me feeling pretty and halfway human. I got this inspo from the Kardashians (see, I'm still basic AF). Whenever I watch old episodes of *KUWTK*, they are always in sweatpants, yet they look so cute and put together! It's because their hair and makeup is always flawless. So whenever someone asks me what my quarantine style was or, better yet, what my maternity style was: it was loungewear with glam. There is nothing that kills my ego more than catching a glimpse of my red puffy rosacea'd face in the mirror. Doing my makeup every day just ensured that there were no accidental unflattering reflection sightings.

Do your hair: One thing I did that was an absolute game changer was highlight my hair. Because of Covid, I didn't get my hair done for months. Then when I found out I was pregnant, I just assumed it was too dangerous. So I went a few more months without doing my hair. Halfway through my pregnancy, I started to ask around, and it turns out like 99.99 percent of women continue to color their hair throughout their pregnancies! I asked my doctor and read some articles and it turns out, highlighting your hair is totes fine and I was just being overly cautious. I'll admit I was overly cautious not only for the sake of my baby's health but also because I didn't feel like giving the trolls another reason to attack me. So I waited until the end of my second trimester, and let me tell you, it made the biggest difference in my self-esteem. Saying goodbye to my mousy dirty-dishwater natural hair color fully revived me. I felt sexy and glamorous. I didn't realize how much I rely on my hair color to make me feel alive. So if you're a pregnant woman struggling to feel like yourself, give your hair a little color or a new cut or some braids. Just don't cut it all off. I had that urge during my pregnancy and quickly realized that a muted light brown bob was not going to do my plump body any favors.

Spray tans: Another game changer. Just hold your nose and try not to take in the fumes. I self-tanned myself with different lotions and sprays. Watching my body quickly balloon up each day freaked me out, and giving myself a little DIY tan was basically me tricking myself into thinking I finally had the "pregnancy glow" everyone talks about, which I think is bullshit, by the way. It's super sweet for people to tell me I had the glow, but honestly, it was not pregnancy, it was my bronzer and highlighter. And maybe an Instagram filter. Who came up with the pregnancy-glow phenomenon? Most pregnant women I know absolutely did not feel glowy whatsoever. Let's look at some of the side effects of pregnancy: adult acne, stretch marks, melasma, pigmentation changes, weight gain, gas and bloating, bleeding gums, hemorrhoids, swollen everything. What part of any of that sounds glowy? All this "pregnancy glow" talk does is make pregnant women feel bad about themselves that they don't have the pregnancy glow. So can we stop with this now?! Until then I recommend self-tanner, bronzer, and highlighter. You're welcome.

Smize: When I was pregnant, I acquired three new chins. Pregnancy face is a very real thing—it's super plump and super round. Any photo I saw of myself where I was open-mouthed, showing all my teeth, and smiling . . . I cringe (I maybe made my friends delete them). I just looked like a very pregnant adult Cabbage Patch kid, if that visual helps. And I am so here for smizing. Probably always will be.

· CHAPTER 7 ·

We (Almost) Bought a Murder House

Call me cray, but I've always loved moving. That might sound weird coming from a homebody, but I've lived all over Los Angeles in different types of apartments, from contemporary condos to high-rise lofts to Spanish duplexes to Venice Beach shacks. There is just something so exciting about a new start, especially when you're leaving that tiny shack with no natural light for a slightly less tiny shack with a little more light. Your twenties are basically a series of moves that lead you from sucky apartments to less sucky apartments, until you're in a place you actually like.

My big move was leaving the West Hollywood apartment I lived in for four years, the one you probably saw on *Vanderpump*, and buying my first home with Beau. Most people would rather get five root canals than pack boxes and move, but I love it. It helps that I love decorating and turning my Pinterest boards into actual rooms. I wouldn't want to pack and move once a year, but I'm here for moving every few years, as long as you're upgrading in some way. Buying my first home with Beau was a major upgrade . . . if only I knew that I would lose all my jobs right after we moved in. Actually, I'm glad I didn't know, because then Beau and I would probably still be sitting on the couch in my old apartment with a baby. Not the end of the world, but still. Sometimes ignorance helps you buy your dream house.

I love our home and was so excited to move, but I had no idea that my old apartment would really be the last place I'd live where I felt totally carefree. If I knew that, I probably would have savored my last months there a little more. Now I live with a man who leaves his beard trimmings in the sink and refuses to shut kitchen cabinet doors. One day when I was pregnant and needed to distract myself from the sight of Beau's beard trimmings, I spent a solid two hours scrolling through old photos and videos from when I was single in my apartment, and boy did I take that shit for granted. I didn't have a care in the freaking world. Life was literally all about getting hammered on wine, shopping, OOTDs, and traveling. My apartment represented a time when I was so selfishly and delightfully focused on living my best life. I was always coming from or going somewhere, always packing for a trip, or unpacking from a trip. Some of my best memories are just of me alone with my dogs and a bottle or two of Prisoner wine staining my white couch. I will always cherish that time. My couch is still stained, but now it's with baby spit-up.

I was so excited to move into an actual house with Beau—one that had central air!—that I didn't bother to give my apartment a proper goodbye. I could have had one last night alone there and done some sort of ritual or séance before leaving, but that didn't happen. I'm just glad that apartment is immortalized on television. If old *Vanderpump* episodes come on, I can relive my single days by watching myself in my old apartment. It feels like I was a completely different person when I lived there. I don't know if it's Covid, or the Canceling, or having a baby, but I feel like I had to grow up really quickly during 2020. Life got way more serious and way more stressful than I expected it to, and fast. It's so funny how we are always in a hurry to get to the next step, and we completely skate over how great the present is. So the moral here is: embrace your single days and your little apartment and your wine nights, because once they're gone, they're gone, bitches!

In *Next Level Basic*, I wrote about my dream to one day live in the Los Feliz murder house, which is just what it sounds like: a haunted house in LA where people were killed. When we started looking for homes, I begged Beau to live in a haunted house with me, but nothing I could do or say got him on board with my plan. Not only did he refuse to live in a house with ghosts, he made me throw out all my Ouija boards, which was devastating. He even made me toss out a little Ouija board magnet! He's terrified of them, which means he actually believes in them. I live for Ouija boards and the undead and creepy sounds coming from the attic. One of my Khaleesis made me a bedazzled Ouija board and gave it to me on one of my book tour stops, and it's one of the most thoughtful gifts I have ever received. I secretly kept it, and it's hidden where Beau will never find it (I know you're reading this, Beau, don't hate me). I know marriage is about honesty and trust, but it's a bedazzled Ouija! I have to draw a line somewhere.

A murder house was obviously out of the question, but a couple of months after we bought our home, someone sent me a side-by-side photo of the view from the Los Feliz murder house and the view from the back of my house, and THEY LOOK IDENTICAL. Is that coincidence?! Maybe I subconsciously realized they were similar because the second I walked into my house, I knew that I wanted it. It was only the third house we looked at, and Beau thought I was absolutely insane to pull the trigger without looking at a million options. I'm of the mind that when you like something, you may as well go for it. Otherwise, all the other options will just put a cloud of doubt in your head. I mean, the wedding dress I chose was the second one I tried on, and then I didn't bother trying on any more after that. Why complicate a good thing? I didn't get to wear the dress, but whatever. I will eventually!

I remember the day we first saw our home so clearly. It was November 30, 2019. The drive up to the house is all narrow streets through the hills, and it's windy AF. We pulled up, and the outside of the house had so much character. It's this beautiful Spanish colonial 1920s house that has a tile mosaic that spells *Bienvenidos* out front. When I walked in, it felt like so much history went down there. Like, being in my house makes me feel like I'm a part of Hollywood history. It was one of the original Hollywoodland homes built in the 1920s, and the neighborhood was basically the original Hollywood Hills. Supposedly you can see the side of our house in the 1956 horror movie *Invasion of the Body Snatchers*, and someone said that Groucho Marx used to live in the house, but I can't verify that because supposedly he bought it under a business name. Sadly I couldn't find any deaths or murders at the house, so no ghosts to report, yet.

I had never been in a house quite like it. It's three stories with a haunted house–like layout. What I mean by "haunted house–like" is that there are a bunch of staircases, and the house is broken up into different areas. It's the opposite of the current open-floor-plan trend. I love a good open-floor plan, but I love haunted house vibes more. I was even more sold when I was told that the house was designed so that every room overlooks the canyon. A good view was on the top of my priority list, so this was a no-brainer. Views just put me in a good mood because they make me feel like I'm on vacation, unless the view is of an alleyway with a dumpster or a Taco Bell, obvs. But if I look out our windows I can pretend I'm in Tuscany, which was a major plus during Covid.

I knew our house was *the one*, but it wasn't perfect. It was going to require a lot of work. I mean, the whole house was cherrywood inside. Like, ew. No offense if you're into cherrywood, but I'm not sure why you would be, unless you're a 1970s businessman whose office smells like cigarettes and whiskey, or a lumberjack. Cherrywood is just not my fave unless it's like, in a mountain lodge. So all the walls needed to be repainted, the kitchen had a huge gaudy pizza oven that barely worked and took up like 40 percent of the space, and some of the bathrooms needed to be redone. It was going to be a project, but I was sold. Beau took a little more time to warm up to it, but not *that* much time. Our HGTV *House Hunters*

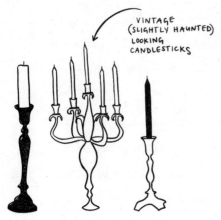

VINTAGE
(SLIGHTLY HAUNTED)
LOOKING
CANDLESTICKS

episode would have been the most boring one in the history of the series. There were no arguments and no drama. I was just super decisive, and once he understood how right I was, we decided to go for it.

Deciding to buy a house is exciting, but the *actual* buying process is a nightmare that I never want to experience again. The whole time we were going through it I just kept thinking, *Why wasn't I taught about this in high school?!* Like, why did I have to learn how to bake blueberry muffins and doughnuts in home economics? Home ec class should've taught us how to buy a freaking house. It's complicated, it takes forever, and it's competitive. Once the whole process was over, I was like, "That's it, we're living in this house forever." Once I got pregnant, I realized that the house was charming, but it was the opposite of baby-friendly. There are literal hazards everywhere. There are steep staircases everywhere, it's on a cliff, there are old-timey vents she could stick her fingers in. When I lived alone, I pretty much just had to worry about things like passing out in a pizza box or my cable going out in the middle of an episode of *RHONY*. Suddenly every staircase, window, balcony, electrical outlet, and sharp object

CHANDELIERS
ARE A <u>MUST</u>

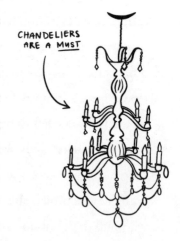

seemed terrifying, and not the fun haunted house kind of terrifying either.

I will say that moving in together provides a cold, hard lesson in compromising, especially when it comes to decorating. Beau and I both have such distinct senses of style, and they are *not* the same. My apartments have always had girly Marie Antoinette vibes. If I could live in something that resembled Versailles, I would. I'm so here for all that gaudy crap. I've always had the same sky-blue walls, white furniture, gold accents, and furry pillows and blankets. I loved my previous place so much, I even modeled my tour set after my apartment. I love any piece that my grandparents would've owned. I think I like honoring traditional style

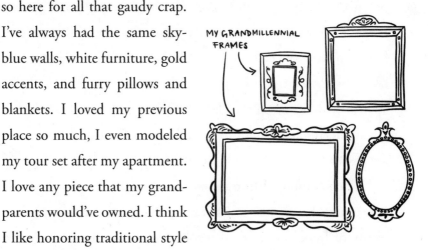

MY GRANDMILLENNIAL FRAMES

in that sense, and then spinning the style into something a bit more eclectic. When I was researching decorating ideas for the house, I came across the term *grandmillennial*. A grandmillennial is someone who has an appreciation for the detail in older homes, like crown molding, original hardwood floors, or chandeliers. That is *so* me. I've always joked that when it comes to my wardrobe, my personal style is "granny chic." Now I have a term to describe my interior design style: a combination of granny and millennial.

I did a lot of the design, but I will give credit where credit is due. Beau has a great sense of home-decor style. That was one of the first things that impressed me about him. Yes, it was very different from mine, but I appreciated all the detail he put into his Spanish-style apartment. It was like a thoughtful mix of vintage, wood, and industrial pieces. Everything in his home had a story. Like the 1800s steamer trunk he bought, restored, and turned into a TV console. Or the creepy statue of two trolls that was gifted to him in Italy. I actually love the scary trolls, and they're one of the items I did not make him hide away. There's also the silver handcrafted dagger from Baghdad that an ex-girlfriend gave him, which I am cool enough to allow him to display in our home. See I *can* be chill. Also, all the art on his walls in his old apartment was also painted by him! Funny tidbit right there, he's a really talented painter. The thing is . . . most of his paintings are nudes.

When we moved into the house, that was a major source of contention. He wanted to put his art all over the walls, and I had plenty of freak-outs where I would have to explain why I didn't want paintings of his ex-girlfriends' naked bodies in my house. I MEAN GIVE ME A BREAK. He truly didn't get it. Any paintings of anything else were very much welcome: a turtle, a teapot—I don't care. I love his art; I just don't love his ex-girlfriends' bare butts. It took like four arguments for him to understand that it just wasn't going to happen. I think he eventually gave up. Boys can be so dumb. The point is, decorating a home together when you have two distinct styles teaches you how to compromise (not when it comes to nude paintings of exes though). Beau wanted to display all his LEGO sculptures on our shelves, which was another hard

no from me. He has his own
room to decorate however he
wants, so please don't feel bad
for him. I also forced him to
keep all of his Rams decor in
the garage instead of displaying
it. He actually has a banner so
big it takes up a quarter of the
garage wall, so, no thank you.
Despite all of that, I think I'm
pretty skilled at compromising.

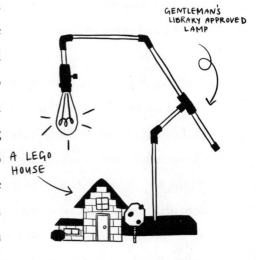

GENTLEMAN'S
LIBRARY APPROVED
LAMP

A LEGO
HOUSE

I took his opinion into consideration on every last thing we put
into this house. I really wanted to decorate the house in a way that
can only be categorized as "Versailles haunted house chic." Did I
do that? Not completely. So you see, I don't always get my way 100
percent. If it's 95 percent, I can live with that.

I allowed Beau to have an opinion about every single piece
I chose—I mean *we* chose—for our home. As much as I wanted
my house to look like a haunted house that Marie Antoinette
threw up in, I was very into creating a style together. I also
wanted him to feel comfortable and at home, instead of feeling
like he was walking around in a princess palace. So for every
"girly" piece I picked out, I also chose a "masculine" one. I made
sure that each room had some element of dark brown leather. I
incorporated mixed metals, industrial pieces, and vintage iron-
work, and I love the way it turned out. I feel like one personal
style can sometimes be a bit one-dimensional, but when you're

blending two personal styles together, the outcome can be so layered and interesting.

There were a few areas of the house that we had to split up. I designed and decorated the nursery without asking for any input. The way I look at it, the nursery wasn't even for the baby, it was for me! I mean, our baby isn't even going to remember it, and I'm the one who's in there all the time feeding her and rocking her and staring at her like a stalker. So basically what I'm saying is that I designed a nursery that is a room I would always want to hang out in, hence my French-country-chic nursery. I gave Beau free rein to design and decorate the "maid's quarters."

Before you crucify me, I did not make up that name, and I feel weird even typing it. "Maid's quarters" is what the Realtor called it when she sold us the house, and no, we do not have a maid living there. Maybe Groucho Marx had a maid living there, so blame him! It's basically a separate mini living area off our kitchen with a mini bedroom, den, and bathroom. It's not mini as in the ceilings are three feet tall, but it's small. It also has its own set of stairs, so I imagine back in the day, that's where Groucho's "maid" slept, hence the name. Anyway, giving Beau free rein to do what he wanted with that area was my gift to him. He turned it into what he calls the "gentleman's library." He thinks the term *man cave* is tacky, so it's a library, I guess, even though there isn't a single book in there. It also serves as our guest room, but for the most part, it's where Beau retreats to watch his sports or play video games. I will give him credit and say he did an A+ job decorating it. It does have a moody vintage library feel, which is very different from my Marie-

Antoinette-meets-country-cottage feel. So, see, compromise! I got the nursery, he got the gentleman's library/guest room/maid's quarters/whatever room.

Once we settled in, I realized that I am the absolute worst neighbor ever, and Beau is the absolute best, which makes me supes insecure. I've always kept to myself. When I come home, I don't want to feel obligated to talk to someone about their oak tree or the weather or whatever. I have always felt like socializing where you live is like shitting where you eat, because then you never really get a break to just not say hello to someone or keep to yourself. You have to stop and talk, even when it's the last thing you want to do. When I was single at my last apartment and going through my "year of yes," I made a decision to change my ways and befriend my neighbors. I actually very much enjoyed getting to know them! However, it did make it awkward when they were constantly having big group apartment barbecues and I just wanted to have some me time. I would sometimes sneakily close my blinds, keep the TV volume low, and pretend I was sleeping, just so I wouldn't get pressured to go to the barbecue and socialize. It took a lot of effort to do nothing.

Once Covid kept us all isolated, my neighbor-phobia changed. I would have loved a neighborhood barbecue now and then. Beau has always been one of those people who organized those big group apartment parties and activities. He knew every neighbor, hung out with them, threw parties with them. So when we moved into our new house, it was no surprise that he introduced himself and made friends with everyone on the block before we got the last box in the door. I, on the other hand, did not. I introduced myself, but that was about it. I actually get really overwhelmed when it comes to making new friends. It takes me a while to open up and get to know someone. I know that seems weird since I've made a living off of constantly opening up on television. Maybe that's exactly why I'm like that though. I do that for work (or I did), so when I'm finished with work, I just want to be alone. I can be quite shy, and I love being a recluse.

During Covid, Beau would have socially distanced happy hours with our neighbors. He would open our garage and sit on our side of the street drinking a White Claw, and our neighbors would open their garages and sit on their sides of the street with whatever they were drinking. Beau still gets annoyed with me that I don't participate or make a bigger effort, and he brings it up about twice a month. He'll ask me to socialize with people on the block, to which I reply, "I don't even get to see most of my friends and family because of Covid, plus I was canceled and branded a racist, so I'm feeling extra vulnerable, and you want me to make more of an effort with complete strangers who might already believe all those things they read about me?!" My biggest insecurity is that my whole neighborhood read the news articles about me and now think they have a KKK member as their next-door neighbor. This is still obviously a sore subject. I mean, at least Beau is there to represent our household as a good and kind citizen. I'll stay behind the blinds and peer out occasionally, like a *normal* person!

I think 2020 was pretty much the year everybody tried to make their home into a little sanctuary, since we were all stuck there

24-7. I just happened to move into a completely new house, where I got to live out my basic bitch fantasy of decorating my dream not-quite-haunted house with glittery chandeliers and spooky-yet-girly accents. Getting the house together actually helped me climb out of rock bottom, since it gave me something else to do besides doom-scroll through Twitter and thinking about my lost job(s) and falling into a black hole of despair! So, yeah. Decorating is great.

Rock-Bottom TAKEAWAY

Even if you're single and living in a tiny apartment with no central AC, embrace that shit because those might just be your last days of pure freedom before you settle down and sign a marriage certificate and a mortgage. I am thankful AF to have a house, but home is really where your couch and your dogs and your wine and your TV are, so don't beat yourself up if you haven't found your "dream home" yet. When you *do* find your home, and if you're sharing it with a partner, make sure you compromise (even if it's just a little) so that both people feel like it's theirs. Also, try to find a house with a man cave/lady cave/gentleman's library so that your partner can decorate it with all the things you hate! Decorating in general is a good way to pull yourself out of a funk, so even if it's just rearranging the chairs in your studio apartment, give it a try.

Stassi's Fave Decor

I love our home, and being pregnant and quarantined gave me plenty of time to wander around deciding which rooms and statement pieces I loved the most. Now that it's Hartford's house too, I love it even more. So here are a few of my favorite things about the house.

The dining room: I love a good open-floor plan just as much as the next person, since you can't beat that when it comes to entertaining, but there is something so romantic and old-school about an actual dining room. I live for a good dining room. It makes me feel like I'm in *Downton Abbey* or *Pride and Prejudice* or something. I realize my dining room doesn't make up even like 10 percent of the *Downton Abbey* dining room, but still. It just feels so traditional and bougie. I totally fantasize about teaching my daughter all her table manners in the dining room. Ironically, our dining room was the absolute last room to come together, so I hated going in there for a long time. It was the only room that I had to take the time to be in, live in, and feel out before I figured out how to decorate it. One of the first things I found for the house was a gold vintage chandelier. I knew I wanted a big round table, because I feel like round tables are so welcoming and efficient at keeping guests included in one conversation. We got a black semigloss table, and I found these rich peacock-colored dining chairs with black and gold detail. It's very New Orleans. For many months, it was just the table, chairs, and chandelier. I couldn't figure anything else out for the room until one day when I was Pinteresting haunted houses, as per usual, and I saw an old-school gallery wall in one of the photos. That's when it hit me! I had so many of my grandmother's pieces of art from her home. They are all in antique gold frames, and once I put them all up, an eclectic gallery wall came together perfectly. I am so proud of that room now. The dining table ended up looking like the most ideal spot for a séance. My mom says the gallery wall reminds her of Disney's Haunted Mansion ride, and my friends joke that the room looks perfect for Halloween all year round, so, mission accomplished.

The chandeliers: When I think about my favorite pieces in the house, each one is a chandelier. I am 100 percent a chandelier queen. I need a cool vintage chandelier in every room, otherwise I'm just not inspired. See? I'm a grandmillennial to the core. I was a little insecure in the beginning that it might be a little too gaudy or tacky to have statement chandeliers in every room, but that was only a fleeting thought that I quickly squashed. Chandeliers make me so happy, and what is more basic and perfect than that?

The nursery: My nursery became the most comforting part of the house before my daughter was even born. I wrote most of this book from the nursery. At first I set up an office with all my Stassi memorabilia to inspire me. People have made me candles with my face on them, ornaments, and bedazzled wine bottles and journals. Despite all the amazing decor and gifts, I never worked in the office. Instead, before Hartford came along, I would bring my computer, an iced tea, and my dog Refund, and we'd sit in the nursery in the glider chair I purchased for breastfeeding and reading bedtime stories. Since my baby was the main thing that kept me from spiraling into a stage-ten depression during 2020, I felt so comforted working from her room. I did have people come to install iron gates over her windows because I'm terrified of someone creeping through her window and kidnapping her. When the installer walked into her nursery, he said, "Whoa, this is a creepy nursery. It's like Old Europe. I could see you walking in to find your kid levitating or something in here." SO, BASICALLY I NAILED THE NURSERY.

The office: The most basic part of the house has to be my office. I mean, it's like a semi shrine to . . . myself. Okay, before you judge me, let me explain. It's not like I have giant canvas modeling photos or glamour shots of myself. I'm not Lady Gaga. I just felt like I earned the right to hang a framed photo of *Next Level Basic* making the *New York Times* bestseller list, and a cool and heavy AF wall hanging from my podcast tour at the Fillmore in New Orleans (it's made out of stones from the location). There also might be a cutout photo of my head from the time I rode as the grand marshal in a Mardi Gras parade. I also get to display the amazing gifts that Khaleesis have brought me at meet and greets. Yes, a shrine to yourself is cringey, but it helps keep me from feeling like my world ended because I was canceled. It reminds me that I've accomplished a lot, and that there is still support out there. You know what, I think everyone should have a mini shrine of their accomplishments in their homes. It does wonders for your self-esteem. It's perfectly acceptable to make manifest/vision boards, so why shouldn't we also make "things we're proud of" boards?! Everyone needs a little confidence booster here and there, so why not find at least a corner of a closet to dedicate to yourself? Put up photos of things you're proud of. It could be your diploma, a photo of your hot bod, your children's artwork, whatever it is that you want to brag about!

Ten Ways to Own Being a Homeowner

1. Trust your gut: If I didn't go with my gut and buy the second or third house we looked at, who knows what would have happened? We would have waited, I would have been fired from all my jobs, a pandemic would have hit, and there we would be, jobless, living in my old apartment with a baby sleeping in the shoe closet, with Beau riding around LA on his scooter looking at homes no one would sell us because I didn't have a job! So, go with your gut.

2. Beware of critters and creatures: When we moved in, I knew we'd have to do construction on my closet, so I stored my shoes, including my Gucci loafers that are furry on the inside, in plastic boxes. Fast-forward a few months, and we ended up having a major moth infestation, like our whole kitchen was swarming with moths. It was a nightmare. It was so disgusting we had to stay with

Katie and Tom while we had the house sprayed. Anyway, when the infestation ended, we would still see a few moths downstairs (far from the kitchen) but we didn't know where they were coming from. Lo and behold, I opened my box of furry Gucci loafers and there were like one hundred dead moths in the fur and tons of eggs all over the shoes. Like, is that where the infestation began? It looked like a horror movie, and I ultimately had to throw them out. The moral is, beware of infestations, and also I'm never wearing loafers with furry insides again.

3. Prepare for disaster: This one isn't even funny. You think people just buy a house and move in? Hell no! Just expect things to break and go wrong and implode and cost three times as much as you think and take ten times as long. And then just enjoy the process!

4. Beware of your partner's bad habits: Another warning. If you move in with a partner, get ready to tolerate all kinds of annoying habits: open drawers and cabinets, boxers left on the floor instead of in the hamper, loose change all over your beautiful antique entry table, crumpling the bathroom towel in a ball instead of hanging it back up. Your partner could be perfect in every way, but bad habits will emerge, so get ready.

5. Decorate patiently: I am supes impatient, and I wish I'd shown more restraint when decorating and finding pieces for our home. Instead, I got excited and rushed in, and there are a few things I wish I could replace but can't because it would be wasteful. Go slowly and take your time furnishing and decorating your home, that way you'll have less regrets.

6. Beware the inspection: Are you sensing a theme here? There is a lot to be scared of when buying a home. Beau spent hours going through every page of our inspection report as if he were studying for the LSAT. With old houses, there's so much fear they'll come back and say, "In five years, your whole house could implode," which they kind of do. So prepare yourself, especially if you're buying an old house.

7. Two words: *rugs* and *chandeliers*: Since I'm preaching patience when it comes to decorating, I've discovered that all you really need in a room is a great rug and a statement chandelier. Start with those two pieces and you'll be set. Who needs a couch when you have a comfy, cool, fuzzy rug? Add a fancy-ass chandelier and you'll have a minimalist glam vibe.

8. Give yourself an end-of-the-day reward: My favorite way to celebrate on the first night in a new home is with pizza and champagne. Figure out what your reward is, and looking forward to it will help you get through the actual move.

9. Have a signature house scent: People have signature perfume scents, so why not make your house have a signature scent? And I do not mean your great-granny's musty flea market scent. I mean get scented candles that you love that become *the* smell when people come into your home. It can be baking scents, holiday smells, or florals, if you're into that.

10. Create a mood: I am so about mood boards. You can go old-school with scissors and magazine cutouts, or use Pinterest. It doesn't have to all be photos of furniture or rooms, you can add fashion photos because you like the color palette, photos of your fave city, or a picture of a fish in the ocean if you want a beachy vibe. It helps get you in the right mind-set to decorate.

CHAPTER 8

From Bridezilla to (Covid) Bridechilla

I spent most of my life thinking I was going to be the most relaxed, laid-back bride. Laugh all you want, but like I mentioned earlier, I didn't grow up imagining what my wedding dress would look like or making scrapbooks about coordinating the napkins with the floral arrangements. Matching my shoes with the wedding cake topper has never been a personal fantasy of mine. Of course, over the years I *thought* about what my wedding might be like. I'm only human, plus I do love fashion and anything that glitters (shout out to my engagement ring). Guys think about their future wedding from time to time too, whether they admit it or not. What I'm saying is that I just never obsessed about what my wedding would be like, which is why I thought I would be such a chill bride-to-be.

But then I got engaged.

I guess I always thought that I was the opposite of someone like Brittany Cartwright, who imagined what her wedding would be like from birth. She probably started planning it in the freaking womb. Brittany fully admits that she had a life-size bride doll as a kid, and it was her most treasured possession. She always knew she wanted the venue to be at the Kentucky Castle in Versailles, Kentucky. She knew the themes and the colors she wanted to have, she fantasized about the apps. Did she imagine Hooters waitresses serving chicken wings? Who knows. I never thought I would be a monster bride-to-be, but then Beau put a ring on my finger and unleashed a demon. It's all his fault.

In case you're not aware, a Bride*chilla* (a term I discovered through the Betches Instagram account) is one who, instead of being an outright devil, does things like send passive-aggressive texts telling her bridesmaids she's totally cool with them wearing short dresses instead of long ones even though she just thought they would all look better in photos if they had on long dresses but NBD it's fine, go ahead and wear minidresses no one will care *even though she asked you to wear long dresses.* She never gets outright aggressive or mean, but she's a little scary with the side-eye when something doesn't go her way. She's somehow able to Zen out and not lose her shit though, remaining totally chill despite the fact that she is actually a burning cauldron of stress inside because she's planning a fucking wedding.

I did have a major Bridezilla moment pretty early on in my wedding planning, before the pandemic came along and basically sent all brides across the planet home to cry in isolation over their lost deposits. Before that happened, I knew as soon as I got engaged that I wanted my bridesmaids to wear all white. Actually, I originally didn't even *want* bridesmaids (see, totes Bridechilla!). My friends bullied me into it. I had seen so much drama with bridesmaids over the last few years, and it's also a lot to ask of a friend, but these bitches *wanted* to be put through hell for me. I agreed to do it, and then I realized that I couldn't just have a small wedding party of, like, two bridesmaids because I have quite a few best friends. I like to keep my circle small, but within that circle they are all my best friends. So, the moral of the story is: I realized I was going to have nine freaking bridesmaids.

As soon as I accepted my fate, I knew right away that I really wanted them all in white, with different silhouettes. White is chic AF. They could wear lace or velvet or chiffon—I didn't care as long as it matched the cool white/ivory vibe I envisioned. I was very specific about this. Lala was one of the bridesmaids, and she was also getting married a few months before me. We were in New York for BravoCon (basically Comic-Con for Bravo superfans, but more on that later), and I remember talking to her about my very chill-but-mandatory color-coordinated silhouette rule, and she commented that she would never allow anyone else to wear white to her wedding, but she would wear a white dress to mine if she had to. She literally said that to me. Remember this.

Cut to the next day, and Lala's stylist comes to my hotel room to get her ready for BravoCon that night. Once Lala is finished getting ready and out of the room, I'm alone with her stylist, who says she needs my measurements since I am one of Lala's bridesmaids. And then she says, "You guys are all going to be in white." Bridechilla immediately left the building and I lost my shit, going off on this poor stylist and yelling, "She said she wanted blush or metallics! She thinks white is a terrible fucking idea!" The stylist said she had just spoken to Lala, and she wanted white. This was literally the only thing I had figured out about my wedding, and so what the actual eff? I went off so hard I think her stylist was scared of me. She went to get Lala, and when she returned Lala fought back, defending her decision and telling me I was pathetic for caring, and I lost my shit all over again. Ah, to be young and naive and pissed off about a dress color!

The next day Lala came to me and said that she told her stylist not to have her bridesmaids wear white dresses, and then she also added that I was insane for getting so angry. I do feel (kind of) bad that I went so hard, but at the time it was important to me. I love fashion and aesthetics and decorating so much, and I had such a clear vision. I needed to defend myself. Still, ages after the fact, and after both our weddings were derailed by Covid, I feel like I need to use this book to very publicly apologize to Lala because that bitch *let* me get what I wanted. So . . .

Dear LaLa,
   I will **NEVER** forget (no matter how much wine I've had) how you so generously let me win our bridesmaid throwdown. That fight could have gotten ugly <u>AF</u> — hair could have been pulled, eyelashes could have been taken off, and boobs could have been punched. Instead, you were a damn queen and I am forever in your debt. Thanks for letting me go full Bridezilla.

All my love,
Stassi

Now I look back on my Bridezilla moments and laugh. Once weddings were canceled, my only wish was to actually even get to have a wedding. Beau and I had been planning an amazing Rome wedding for the fall of 2020 (LOL but also WTF). When I found out we would have to postpone, I told my wedding planner that I didn't even care if we had to eat pizza off paper plates, I just wanted to one day make it to Italy for the wedding. I didn't care if my dress ripped, the music skipped, and everyone got food poisoning (provided we all survived), I decided I was going to be the chillest most thankful bride ever. How many people got married over Zoom, or lost their deposits, or eloped instead of doing their dream destination wedding? The answer is: a freaking lot.

Lala was devastated when her April 2020 wedding didn't happen. I think people with 2020 weddings planned during the early months of Covid had the hardest time dealing with it because they had to cancel them so suddenly. There wasn't a lot of time to digest what was happening. It definitely helped that I had several months to process everything. I mean, Lala's bachelorette party trip was supposed to be the last week of March 2020. I remember when that got canceled, it felt huge. It made the pandemic very real. Lala and I have gone through such similar life changes. Neither one of us got our 2020 weddings, which makes our (or my) Bridezilla fight about the white bridesmaid dresses seem even sillier. I mean, I would love it if the pandemic never existed and we both got to be as Bridezilla and/or Bridechilla as we wanted, but instead we both ended up with something better: we both got pregnant with baby girls.

As much as I wanted my dream Italian wedding, part of me feels like weddings had become a bit of a circus, and Covid kind of hit the reset button on that in some ways. We were living in a world where we were all after the biggest and best wedding, constantly trying to outdo each other, constantly comparing dresses or cakes or venues, and I was very much part of that problem. I mean, I was planning a televised Italian wedding, so yeah, I'm definitely guilty of pushing the whole giant wedding spectacle. Once Covid happened though, couples were forced to refocus on themselves. Traveling was out of the question, and big guest lists were banned.

What mattered was just being able to get married, instead of having a dress worthy of *Vogue*. This refocusing was definitely true for me and Beau.

Once I accepted the fact that our big televised Italian wedding 2020 was probably not happening, I didn't feel the need to rush it. Turns out it was very important to Beau that we got married before our daughter, Hartford, came. Who knew he was so old-fashioned? I, on the other hand, must have still been rebelling from my strict all-girls Catholic school upbringing by getting a kick out of having a baby out of wedlock. Oh, the nuns would've died. Once I realized that Covid could go on indefinitely though, I also wanted to get married in 2020 and not wait. I didn't know when our dream wedding would happen, and I just wanted to be married to Beau, so why let Covid prevent us from doing just that? The fact that it was so important to Beau made a small ceremony seem sweet, instead of seeming like a curse.

We held out hope for as long as we could, since our wedding invitations had gone out and our venues had been booked. I didn't have a Covid crystal ball, telling me when it would all be over, but everyone from our wedding planner to my *Vanderpump* producers were telling me to hold off on canceling. At that time, everyone "knew" someone who had some magical insight into the pandemic. Remember when people said UV light killed the virus? Or that there would be a vaccine by July? Oh, no, wait—vaccines will be ready in September, and then . . . Well, you know how it went. So-and-so's brother was a doctor and they said it would all be over by the fall! Another person's boyfriend's best friend works for some scientist who says we'll be clear by October. Looking back on all that now, I'm literally chuckling out loud. It wasn't until I realized that *if* Covid were to disappear and we'd somehow be able to marry in Rome in October 2020, I'd be seven months pregnant at my wedding. That became a very obvious HELL NO from me.

First of all, I had already gotten two spectacular wedding dresses, which were not exactly maternity style. And second of all, there was no way I was going all the way to Italy to not drink the wine. That was a dealbreaker right there. Postponing the wedding because I had just been blessed with the greatest gift of all time made it way easier to deal with. Kind of like how my pregnancy got me through being canceled, my pregnancy helped me not feel sorry for myself when it came to my wedding. The prospect of being a mom was way more exciting to me than a big wedding. So we decided to push our wedding back exactly a year. That would give me nine months to get back to my wedding dress, pre-baby weight. HA! The thought of having our daughter at our wedding was so exciting. I still found myself googling *When will Covid be over?* just in case. Every time I did that, I realized that a Roman fall 2021 wedding might not happen either! So much of my wedding was already paid for, and it would be money down the drain. I know I am definitely not alone in that feeling.

What wasn't normal was that I wasn't just canceling or postponing a wedding—I was postponing a wedding that had been agreed upon by the show that had just fired me. Beau and I had hard-core played ball with Bravo and our producers so that our wedding would be easy for *Vanderpump Rules* to film. We even took our producer with us to Italy on our wedding location scouting trip. We chose a venue, a rehearsal dinner spot, and a hotel that were all filming-friendly, even though they weren't our top choices. And if you're sitting there thinking I should be grateful that Bravo was going to pay for my wedding, think again! Bravo does not and to my knowledge has never paid for a single wedding on any show. Beau and I were paying for our wedding ourselves. So when we had to choose the hotel they wanted, we were paying for that. The wedding venue that would allow us to film? We were paying for that. Even the cast members were going to have to pay for their own flights and hotel. Bravo paid for one thing, and that was to book my wedding venue the day before my wedding date so that production could set up.

So after going through months of planning a wedding that would work for television, to be fired stung in a whole new way. Here we were, left with all these locations we wouldn't have necessarily chosen for our wedding, because we wanted to make it work for Bravo, and Bravo had just let me go. So if there has been disappointment regarding my future wedding, it's that I would've planned things a little differently had I known we wouldn't be filming it. But I get it. I was able to plan a Roman wedding, so I should stop complaining. Maybe a little bit of Bridezilla was still in me after all!

I didn't realize how much I wanted my Italian wedding until I couldn't have it. I did my share of crying, but eventually I decided to think optimistically. By the time we would have our wedding, our baby girl would be able to be our almost-two-year-old flower girl. How dreamy is that? Recognizing that Covid affected so many people in so many more horrible ways also made me realize that yes, postponing or even canceling a big wedding isn't exactly fun, but it's not the end of the world. I still get to marry the love of my life and have a baby. I have a soft mattress and my dogs and pizza and Cinnamon Toast Crunch to get me through, and I did end up having a ceremony, it was just far away from Italy and we hired someone called "the Officiant Guy" (seriously) to, well, officiate.

We were still hopeful that one day we'd get to have our dream Italian wedding, so Beau and I wanted our 2020 preggo ceremony to be as short and uneventful as possible. We accomplished our goal because I'm pretty sure it was over in like three minutes. Oh, and we also did it at my baby shower. Talk about killing two birds with one stone. Who would've thought I'd be okay with a quickie ceremony, but there I was, totally chill. I went from Bridezilla wanting to rip Lala's hair out over a bridesmaid dress color to being a *true* Bridechilla. I think my whole outfit cost a hundred bucks.

The dual shower/wedding idea started when two of my best friends, Taylor Strecker and Taylor Donohue (who got engaged in 2020!), came to visit us. They asked me if I'd be open to having a last-minute baby shower since they were in town. Because of Covid and the Canceling, I hadn't been in the mood to celebrate anything. I didn't want a big baby shower because it felt weird to be so celebratory, and I wanted to be as safe as possible. This was in early September, when I was still quiet and still hadn't rejoined earth (or social media) completely. I realized that if I *was* going to have a baby shower, I would want them there, and this was my only opportunity.

My bestie Katie Maloney, with the help of our friends, planned a socially distanced baby shower within a week. Beau and I figured it would be a great time to get married, since we'd already have our closest friends there. We were looking at it strictly as our civil ceremony, where we made our marriage legal. We'd have to make it legal in the United States before we went to Italy anyway, so why not? Beau was in charge of the whole thing. I told him that if he wanted to marry me that badly, he had to plan it. (I'm a brat, for reelz.) I also demanded that we do a private marriage license (you can do this in California), so that TMZ or Page Six didn't spill the news before we could. I was totes over anything else in my life being leaked to the tabloids.

Beau found "the Officiant Guy" and scheduled him to come to Katie's and perform a quick private ceremony with a confidential marriage license. He was amazing, but it was kind of like the KFC or McDonald's of ceremonies. We didn't tell anyone but Katie what we were actually doing, so halfway through our little shower, we asked everyone to come outside, and—surprise!—we got married in like 180 seconds. Katie surprised me with a little bouquet, but besides that it was just our shower decorations. At first I don't think our friends even believed what was happening, and just like that, we were married, with our little baby in my belly!

With all that had happened in 2020, I wasn't really in the mood to be the center of attention (*so* not me), but we weren't going to let the bad stuff keep us from getting married. Did I ever imagine that I'd make it legal in my best friend's backyard with about ten people during a mini baby shower in a random white maternity dress? Absofreakinglutely not. But 2020 taught me to just roll with everything, and to appreciate the little things. Every time I look at the video of us getting married, I feel so incredibly grateful. Nothing is how I imagined it would be, but it is just as sweet. Maybe sweeter. I think I've realized I have a hidden talent, which is that I'm pretty good at adapting. Plus, on the actual day I turned out to be the most chill bride ever. Who woulda thought?

If you had to cancel or postpone your 2020 wedding (or if you did it via Zoom), I want to start by saying that what happened to you totally sucks and any anger or sadness you felt is *totally* valid. If you wallowed, there is no judgment. We all react to things differently. I just know that I can't handle wallowing and feeling depressed for too long. It's too tiring. I am way better at life when I let things go, and the only way for me to let our 2020 wedding go was to remind myself that the same thing was happening to a whole lot of people around the globe. It's not like I was sitting around watching everyone else have their dream weddings while I couldn't. There was nothing to feel FOMOish about because we all struggled together. Unless you're a Kardashian and you got to go to business meetings in Paris with a private Louvre tour or fly a million people to Tahiti for your birthday. Love the Kardashians, but watching their Instagram stories during Covid made me feel so ridiculously poor and sad. But that's neither here nor there. My main advice is to just hold out hope that one day you'll get your dream wedding, and maybe you already have. Not to sound too pastory, but sometimes, hope is all we got.

And finally, to all those lovely ladies who will soon become Bridezilla fiancées: the next time you get all cray cray and pissed because your cake ended up three tier as opposed to four, or the wrong song got played for your father-daughter dance, just take a few moments to think about all the 2020 brides who didn't even get a wedding. Just feel #blessed you get to have a wedding at all, and chill the eff out.

Rock-Bottom TAKEAWAY

Bridezillas will probably roam the earth until the end of time, but try to remember that at the end of the day, what really matters is that you're married. No one will remember what kind of potatoes or cupcakes you had at your wedding. Would I still love a romantic, dramatic Rome wedding? OF COURSE! Was my life over because I didn't get it? Nope. Like every Covid bride, Bridezilla, and Bridechilla knows, life goes on. And try to remember not to lose your shit about the color of a bridesmaid dress. And if you do, apologize to your bridesmaid later with a nice, public note (hi, Lala).

CHAPTER 9

(Don't) Always Buy the Shoes

On my eighteenth birthday, my mom gave me a sweet card. Inside that card, she left me some horrible financial advice. She wrote down eighteen life lessons for me, and one of them was:

Always buy the shoes, even if you don't have the money.

I mean, WTF kind of advice is that?! Do you know how much trouble that got me into? There were times I could barely pay rent but *I still bought the shoes*! I love my mom, but that was not the sagest advice passed down from a mother to a child. Since that day, and especially throughout 2020, I have learned that, no, you should not always buy the shoes, even if they're sparkly and gorgeous and everything in you is saying *CHARGE MY CARD*.

I don't remember talking about money with my parents growing up. Like most kids, I just noticed that certain people had more of it than others, which I noticed when I saw pools or trampolines or the latest American Girl doll, which was something my parents never got me. I hold a grudge about it to this day. I also knew that my mom didn't have as much money as my dad did, because when they divorced, my dad was in a nicer neighborhood in a bigger home, which equaled more money. When I was a kid, my mom and dad never handed me money just because I asked for it. I had to make As to get an allowance, but then later my little brother could get a C+ and get an allowance, which was so not fair. Once I was old enough to work, my first job in high school was a barista at a coffee shop, and I freaking *loved* the feeling of making my own money. I felt free. It was one of my first memories of feeling awesome and independent. I loved having a job, even if the boss called me into his office one day to show me an infamous paparazzi shot of Britney Spears getting out of a car and supposedly exposing her vagina. Despite that disgusting moment, which actually caused me to quit the job (#FreeBritney), I loved being financially independent.

That feeling never left me. I loved making money doing *Vanderpump* or my podcast or the live *Straight Up with Stassi* shows, and I loved being able to go travel using money that I'd earned by working hard. I depended on no one but myself. It is important to note though, that up until I got fired from basically everything, I had an extremely privileged view of money, in the sense that I believed that no matter what, there were always more jobs to pick up and more money to be made. I didn't spend above my means, but I did sometimes splurge without thinking, because I assumed there would always be another job, if I just hustled.

As many of you know, that is not always the case. Not even close.

What I would give to be able to just pick up jobs whenever I want. It's not always so easy to walk into an interview (or even get an interview) and nail a position. When I had all that quarantine time to sit on rock bottom and look at my life, I felt foolish for ever having such a privileged view of money and work. Now I'm extremely grateful for any job that comes my way. I guess you could say I was a super douche about money before, but then I learned the hard way that opportunities don't just sail into your lap, and shoe purchases sometimes have to be put on the back-burner until you figure your shit out. It's a scary feeling, and one that I'd forgotten about because I felt so secure about where I was in life financially and career-wise. I guess another lesson is: don't ever get too comfortable, because none of us know what's around the corner. That doesn't mean you have to live in terror and stash money under your mattress, but I will just never take work for granted again.

In college I was extremely lucky at first, because my dad helped with the loans I was taking out. Several years after I graduated, I secretly paid off the rest of the loans without telling my dad. Before I was able to do that, during college I devised all kinds of clever/pathetic ways to stretch a buck, like driving across town to Little Caesars for a five-dollar pizza, which I would make last me an entire week. I would eat it cold for days. I mean, does pizza ever really go bad? I don't think so. I would also go to 7-Eleven and look for the protein bar with the highest amount of protein to fill me up. I'm not sure if that was about being frugal or if it was a sign of an eating disorder, so I'll just go with frugal. The bulk of my culinary budget went to cheap, giant, double-decker bottles of crap wine. I never bought regular bottles, only jumbo. That is pretty much all I ate and drank during college, and I wouldn't really recommend it, but it worked for me.

I learned pretty quickly after moving to Los Angeles that going on dates was a solid plan when it came to getting free drinks and meals. I said yes to almost any guy who asked me out back then, because it was a free dinner. Sorry, but it's true. I'm not saying I gave them all a kiss at the end of the night, but I would go to dinner, sit there and talk, and if I didn't like them, that was that.

I could have fun talking to random dudes as long as they weren't gross or boring AF, which they sometimes were. My friends and I did the same thing at clubs. We would wear our fake Herve Leger bandage dresses and hover around the guys who had bottle service until they called us over, and then we'd spend a few hours drinking their chilled vodka and flirting until it was time to go home. I'm pretty sure half the reason we went out at night was to get effed up for free.

To get things like my fake Herve Leger dresses, I would go to a store on Larchmont in Hollywood called LF that used to have massive sales twice a year. Little hussies like myself would wait in a line around the block and nearly claw each other's eyes out once we got inside, so we could nab the best deals. That was the only way I bought clothes, besides doing something truly embarrassing called . . . Model Mayhem. It was a website where anyone could register, and models, photographers, stylists, and makeup artists could find each other for shoots. If it sounds fancy, it was not. It was the most low-grade, unprofessional modeling industry site in the world. What did I know though? I was twenty-one, and I needed cute clothes. I wasn't trying to get on the cover of *Vogue*. So basically a few times I would get booked and I would do a shoot (yes, fully clothed, thanks very much) and my payment would be the clothes I wore. One thing I did not do, but which is very common in LA, is that I did not become a kept woman with a sugar daddy. I did get propositioned once, in college, when one of my good friends at the time invited me to come to some resort with her and some dude and some other dude, who happened to be a somewhat famous magician who I had met exactly once. At first I said yes because I thought it was a fully paid girls' trip, but then she said

I'd be staying in the magician's room, which was a hard no from me. That actually led to a massive fight with my friend, and we were never really close after that. I was insulted. She was basically inviting me to become a kept woman at a resort with a strange guy, which might sound amazing to some people, but I am not about that kind of girls' trip. Plus he was a magician. I loved free dinners and champagne, but not if there were some creepy expectations attached to the deal. I would rather eat my protein bars and drink my jumbo wine alone, in peace.

Throughout the years on *Vanderpump*, we all kept each other in check financially because we started from the same place—broke and working in a restaurant. We would have made fun of each other if someone bought a Ferrari or something once the show got popular. We were all on the same level, so we spent pretty wisely. My biggest splurge early on was hair extensions and Botox. If you watch old seasons, you can see a change in how I looked on the show, because I was making enough to look more polished with highlights and extensions and Botox. I got fillers for a while too, but I stopped. God, I looked so good back then. In season four, you can also see that we were all a little plumper, because we could actually afford food! I am not joking.

I remember when we all got our first big checks, in season three. We had finally started making some money, and I drove to my manager's office to physically pick up the $25,000 check. It was such a dramatic, exciting moment, and I just felt like *Holy shit, I have a five-figure check!* It was such a major moment. I deposited the check and stuck the deposit slip on my refrigerator, which is totally embarrassing, but I was proud. Before that, we would all rotate dresses to save money, if you want to know where we were financially. We were sometimes filming three scenes a day, where you would have to wear three different outfits, and so we became like Sisterhood of the Traveling Dresses so we could save money and not look like we were wearing the same outfit every day of our lives. If you watch the first few seasons very closely, with a magnifying glass and a notepad, you'll see the same dresses make the rounds. We just kept borrowing and trading, hoping no one would notice, and I don't think anyone did. Until now, maybe.

When I think back on the early seasons of *Vanderpump Rules*, I sometimes cringe at my bratty ways, even though audiences loved (and hated) that version of me. In season one, I got pissed because I had a birthday party in Vegas with a bunch of friends (if you read *Next Level Basic* you might remember that this was the trip where I called some of my friends my "B" group, which was incredibly lame, I know). The show paid for two drinks per person plus some food, and I threw a fit because I thought it was my birthday and my friends came out to Vegas and they shouldn't have to pay for a thing. The ones who weren't on the show were not getting paid to be there, plus they had to take off a shift at SUR, so I was trying to defend them. So I did what season-one Stassi always did, I sobbed and locked myself in a bathroom. One of the producers came to the bathroom door and basically said, "Next time, we'll just have your birthday at McDonald's." Her fast-food tough love shut me up real quick. McDonald's can be delicious, but it is no Taco Bell, and I don't really want to have my birthday party there. Maybe if they offer free meals plus bottomless Aperol spritz pitchers all night, but that's it.

Thankfully I married someone who has pretty much the same spending and saving habits as I do. Beau loves to splurge on experiences like travel or dinner, and so do I, so we don't ever fight about a fun night out in West Hollywood or a trip to Marie Antionette's old house, which happens to be Versailles. I probably should have married my opposite when it comes to spending, now that I think about it, because then one person would be like, "Why did you spend eighty dollars on cocktails?" instead of being like, "Let's get another round!" Beau is more mindful than I am when it comes to money though. We actually keep our money separate, so there's fewer reasons to fight. I don't need him knowing about every shoe I buy (because, yes, sometimes I do buy the damn shoes), and he doesn't need me to know about every Yoda figure or *Star Wars* LEGO set or whatever the hell else he buys for his gentleman's library. I don't want anyone to monitor me, because I worked hard so I could have the freedom to do what I wanted with the money I earned. I've always been of the mind that I am responsible for myself, and now of course we have Hartford to think about. I know not to overspend. I'm not out there trying to buy the fanciest shit in the world, especially not after losing all my jobs. I would like to enjoy my life with the money I've earned, and in 2020 and 2021, I learned not to take that money, or the jobs that supplied it, for granted.

As soon as I was fired from *Vanderpump*, I was incredibly thankful that the house Beau and I *had just bought* was on the lower side of our budget. Something told me it would be irresponsible to stretch our budget, especially when you're relying on loans. That might be the only money advice I feel totally confident giving: just because you *can* spend a lot doesn't mean you should. After the Canceling I met with my business manager, who told me exactly how long I could go on without a job before I was truly broke. Like, selling-the-house/moving-in-with-my-mom broke. It was scary to hear, but luckily we discovered that our biggest splurges were all travel related, and with the pandemic no one was traveling anywhere. We saved money because we literally could not leave the house. Once I got over the shock of losing my livelihood, I started thinking of ways I could create a job for myself. In July 2020 I thought of starting a podcast about our life as first-time parents called *The Good the Bad the Baby*, but it was all going to be centered around Beau and become a dad brand, and I would be behind the scenes producing!

Who am I kidding though? I don't just want to be the brains. At first I thought I could be like Kris Jenner and orchestrate this amazing brand for Beau from behind the scenes, but I wanted in on it. It's in my soul to be the talent. I was and am a musical theater nerd, which is a blessing and a curse that never leaves you. I need to be onstage, whether it's TV, an actual stage, or on a podcast. So we worked as a team, came up with the branding and the look and everything else, and launched a podcast. Our lives revolved around being parents, so why not turn our everyday lives into our job?

Rock bottom has a way of making you appreciate every job, and every check that comes your way. It doesn't matter how prepared you think you are, shit can always hit the fan and you can lose everything. I thought I had it all covered. I thought that if *Vanderpump* ended I could continue the podcast or live tours, I had a *Basically Stassi* talk show in the works at Bravo, I had books to write. I thought I'd made sure that if I lost one job, I'd have other sources of income. When every single one of those things went away, I had to come up with a new plan. So I did. Was I wrong for things I said and did? Yes. Am I remorseful? Absolutely. But I still get angry that the answer to those mistakes was erasing all of my hard work and making me unhirable. Like I keep saying, I can be remorseful and also upset about what happened. Now I know that every opportunity matters, and every paycheck. And the next time I am able to get on a plane and take a trip to Rome or Paris or Versailles, I will appreciate the shit out of it, because I now know what it's like to not have that.

This might not be the most likable or sympathetic thing to say, but one thing I refused to curb my spending on, even after that scary meeting with my business manager, was baby stuff. I recognize that's a privilege and it's bratty, but getting cute things for Hartford was all I had to look forward to in 2020. I also looked forward to meeting her, obvs. Being at rock bottom was hard enough, and I wasn't going to let all that change my experience as a first-time mom. It was something I'd dreamed about forever. It's almost like a rite of passage for first-time moms to spend money on stupid shit your baby probably won't ever wear or use. I wanted to have the freedom to decorate her nursery how I always imagined and buy her clothes and toys I always dreamed of getting. I'm not saying I was always right, but dammit, I needed it. When Beau suggested a million times that I should rent a fancy "smart bassinet" called a Snoo instead of buying it, I would always respond, "I worked way too freaking hard for the last however many years to build up to this point where I could provide for my future baby, and that's not going to be taken from me! I'm buying the damn Snoo!" Joke is on me because Hartford didn't like the Snoo, and I wish I had listened to Beau and rented it, but I am not here to give financial advice. I know not to order expensive coffee drinks five times a day, and I taught myself to do my own gel manicures. I go on walks instead of paying for a gym membership. But that's all I've got. If anyone wants to teach me how to invest, I'm all ears.

I will say I had a giant wake-up call losing my income and putting myself in check as far as my attitude toward money, how I make it, and how I save. I wasn't as appreciative as I should have been before, and now I understand that every opportunity and every job matters. I never could have imagined what happened, and I really thought I had all my bases covered. I will definitely teach Hartford about money when she's old enough. My grandma was the most fiscally responsible human being I've ever met, and she was a Capricorn, like Hartford. So I'm hoping my daughter will inherit that astrological gift of being good with money. But real talk, I'm going to make my daughter take money-management classes one day, even if she hates me for it at first. Instead of teaching kids home economics, we need to teach them real world shit. We don't need to learn how to make banana muffins, we need to learn how to achieve a good credit score. Teach us about taxes and car registration and home buying and balancing a freaking budget, not how to deep fry a doughnut hole. I want my daughter to be everything I'm not (or wasn't) when it comes to money, which is responsible, grateful, and able to see that buying a "smart bassinet" isn't always a smart financial decision. And finally, no offense to my mom, I will never tell her to always buy the shoes. I'll advise her to check her accounts, make sure it's a good decision, and *then* buy the shoes. Unless they are to die for. Then, she'll have to decide for herself.

Rock-Bottom TAKEAWAY

First of all, schools need to teach kids and young girls money management and building good credit instead of teaching us how to bake a Bundt cake. Yes it might be boring AF, but if they explained to us that we could actually get cuter outfits or a better house if we were smart about money from day one, we would probably listen! Losing everything will teach you the value of a dollar real quick, and I for one will never cry because my birthday isn't good enough or because I can't get the bassinet I want again. Jobs don't just come around when you need them, and I learned that the hard way. Yes, I take full responsibility, and yes, I was scared and hurt and angry. And yes, I am working every day to make sure that never happens again. So be resourceful, always deposit your checks, and buy the shoes if you must but not if you can't.

CHAPTER 10

Self-Care Sundays
(and Mondays, Tuesdays, Wednesdays, Thursdays, Fridays, and Freaking Saturdays)

Before I was pregnant, my self-care toolkit pretty much consisted of the following:

A couch

A television (plus a remote, obvs)

Snacks (Doritos, Taco Bell, mac 'n' cheese, maybe a salad if I'm feeling healthy)

Iced tea (daytime)

Wine (nighttime, or afternoon, depending how stressed I am)

Sweats

A scented candle (Apple strudel or pumpkin pecan waffle scents from Pure Integrity are my faves, and if you gift me any sort of "fresh laundry" candle I will cut you out of my life.)

Cozy blanket

Fluffy, loyal dogs

Phone on mute

That's pretty much all I needed to feel relaxed and rejuvenated. Beau meditates and writes in a journal, and it works for him, but I just need some junk food, a drink, my dogs, and comfy clothes. And a television, which is the altar of self-care at which I worship. When I got pregnant, I had to delete wine from my list, and replace it with a bunch more things that are way less fun, like root beer. As a boring pregnant person in quarantine, my self-care toolkit became a little more complicated.

OVERSIZED CASHMERE SWEATPANTS

A pregnancy pillow (Have you seen them? They are *huge*.)

Movies I've already watched 29,657 times

Snacks with sugar (Waffles, Cinnamon Toast Crunch cereal *before* some guy found shrimp tails in his box, funfetti cakes, ice cream, Sour Patch Kids— I could go on.)

Sparkling water (I was trying to limit caffeine and this at least felt a little festive.)

Root beer (A poor substitute for a cocktail.)

3XL sweats

Compression socks that match my sweats so I feel chic and monochromatic

Christmas scented candles (even in July)

A phone charger with an extra-long cord

A gel manicure kit

Parenting books

Cozy blankets

My dogs (They would not leave my side, like stalkers.)

Phone on mute

TikTok

Emily in Paris (The most basic bitch show, which was everything I needed at the time.)

Epsom salt bath every night (For pregnancy hemorrhoids, bitches.)

Pampering yourself while pregnant is a woman's solemn right, and we should be able to do it in any way we need to, as long as we're not murdering anyone or doing shots or eating a bunch of cold cuts, which apparently you're not supposed to do. I don't know many pregnant women who consider training for a marathon or climbing Everest a form of relaxation, but I'm sure those maniacs exist. For me, it was all about laziness and alone time. That's not just when I'm pregnant, it's pretty much my lifelong MO. Pregnancy gave me a very good excuse though.

I didn't understand that watching television with my dogs was my personal form of self-care until a few years ago. I was doing my podcast, and I was telling the guest that I was single, since Patrick and I had recently broken up (again). I was telling the guest how I loved being at home all alone so much more than I did when I was in my early-twenties club-rat phase. I was such a little psycho back then, possibly because I hadn't discovered that the way I gain energy and get centered is by being alone. I always thought I was such an extrovert and needed to be out in drunken crowds all the time, but I'm actually pretty introverted. Actually, I think I'm a mixture. I'm an ambivert, which is a real word, BTW. Feel free to google it. Anyways, doing this podcast helped me understand that being an ambivert and having some alone time was very good for my soul.

In the last few seasons of *Vanderpump*, you might (or might not, since you have a life) have noticed that I was rarely in the late-night scenes. We would film dinners and maybe one bar after dinner, but when they wanted to keep rolling at the late-night/ early-morning after-party in the hotel or wherever, I was usually back in my room, asleep. When we filmed trips, the producers always wanted to film the postmidnight moments, because that is when the good (or so bad it's good) shit happens. Everyone was nice and toasted from drinking for hours, and of course that's when the drama starts. When I was doing the show, the producers were pretty understanding about my self-care needs, so usually they let me sleep (off camera), but sometimes they would come in with cameras while I was ordering food or something, just so it didn't seem like Beau and I disappeared for no reason. The producers often tried to convince me to film late-night scenes, but my reply was usually, "We're filming a reality show, and in real life I would never be after-partying in a hotel room. I would be sleeping." It always worked because it was a great excuse, but it also happened to be true.

When I was working and busy with the show and the podcast tour and everything else I was doing before Covid and the Canceling, I used to live for those self-care moments. It was such a luxury to have a day off and enjoy my alone time. In 2020, since we were all at home with little to do but face masks and *Tiger King* (unless you have kids, in which case you would probably have killed for five seconds of self-care), I started to feel like: Is there such a thing as too much self-care? There was so much time for self-care, to the point that I was soon over it. I legit fantasized about being so busy and worn out and just needing a moment to take a breather or something. Honestly, by the end of the year, I wanted to cancel self-care and become busy AF, but that didn't happen.

Of course, self-care *is* important. I just don't need to do it around the clock every single day of the year. Looking back, everything I used to bitch and moan about backfired. I used to beg for some downtime to relax and focus on myself, and then suddenly I was fired from every job I had during a worldwide pandemic. Like I said, relaxing and focusing on myself got old, fast. I didn't realize how much my self-esteem was wrapped up in how much I was working. Even though I might complain about needing a break, I feel good about myself when I'm busy or overwhelmed with work. Needless to say, I wasn't exactly operating at my best since I had nothing to do but stay home and chill, or pretend to chill while the world was in total chaos.

About six months before I got pregnant, I was on the phone with my psychic, Chris Medina. He is literally the best. He predicted that I would have a baby girl. Before that, he predicted Beau, and he foresaw my canceling. If you don't believe me, or if you think psychics are basic bitch BS, here is what he said on my podcast about my career *before* the Canceling:

I feel like there are going to be some issues when it comes to your management or the people that work for you. They are going to drop the ball or they are going to disappoint you in some way, shape, or form. You're going to have more time on your hands. . . . There are a lot of lessons that are going to come into play. . . . There obviously are going to be bumps in the road. Your guides are going to do a real number on pulling you back and saying, "Okay, Stassi, what have we learned so far and how are we going to progress and how do we want to grow, soulfully and as a person, mixed in with your career?" Within the next three years, there isn't anything that will come at you that you can't handle.

He also told me I need to get out of my head, stop pressuring myself, and relax. It felt good to hear him say that. It was almost like I needed to hear some sort of permission to chill out. I spent months feeling bad about myself for having nothing to do, and it gave me such a love-hate relationship with anything having to do with self-care. I wish I could have given myself the permission to go easy on myself. Maybe that's what my version of self-care is now: giving myself permission to just rest, and not feel guilty about it.

It might sound like I minorly had my shit together in 2020 and that I was handling all my stress with Epsom salt baths, but I feel like it's important for me to remind you that I had about 2,384,762,384 breakdowns, give or take. Every week brought new emotions. I went through phases where I felt incredibly resilient and strong, and then weeks where I couldn't sleep at all through-out the night because everything seemed hopeless. I had not-so-

soothing late-night thoughts like: *Will I ever work again? Will I ever get a paycheck again? Will I have to sell my house? Does everyone think I'm awful? When will Covid just be over?* Those are the moments I would have killed for a Xanax, or wine, or both. Obviously being pregnant, that was all out of the question. So moral of the story, I'm still figuring it all out.

One thing that was incredibly zen and relaxing for me was video games. That's right, my self-care sometimes involves a headset and some *Diddy Kong Racing*. My brother, Hunter, has always been a huge gamer, so growing up, he'd occasionally let me play with him. I was really into Nintendo 64. I loved *Super Mario*, *Mario Kart Racing*, *Yoshi's Story*, *Diddy Kong Racing*, and *GoldenEye 007*. I'm so basic I would just pick one of the female characters, Xenia or Natalya. I always got "Most Cowardly" at the end of every *Golden-Eye* game because I'd just find the hiding spots and stay there the whole time until the other players killed each other off, and then I'd pop up and start shooting and win because I was the only one left! That probably reveals something about my personality, but I'll leave it to the psychologists to figure it out. I love *GoldenEye*, but my absolute favorite game has always been PlayStation's *Crash Bandicoot*.

When we first started dating, I told Beau that I loved *Crash Bandicoot*, and he bought it for me since I hadn't played in years. Looking back on it, he probably got it to keep me preoccupied when I become annoying or clingy, which is often. A little video game action can be very relaxing since it's a perfect way to zone out. Instead of thinking about bills or being canceled, I got to think about what type of car I was going to pick to beat everyone in Rainbow Road or Bowser's Castle. I once went through a huge VR (virtual reality) game phase, and got into it again at the start of quarantine. For the first two months, I'd put on my Oculus set and search for games and apps that made me feel like I was traveling. When the virtual vacay was over, I picked games that transported me into a horror movie. Maybe I liked it because these horror movies had nothing to do with the *actual* horror show of 2020. You can choose between escape rooms, haunted houses, or horror movies where you become a character. I'm not going to lie—they are terrifying. You have a VR headset on, so everywhere you turn, you are suddenly inside that setting. Just imagine walking through a very realistic haunted environment with dead people coming at you, and when you turn your head to look behind you, there's a serial killer right there! It's disturbing, and I love it. When I finished passing the time by terrifying myself, I'd search *Paris* or *Rome* and immerse myself in a city across the world. I spent a whole lot of time prepregnancy sipping on wine, with my VR set, strolling the streets of Paris.

When I found out I was pregnant, I got a NordicTrack, because I read in Jessica Simpson's memoir that she lost one hundred pounds after she had her baby just by walking. It's very basic bitch of me, but I love Jessica and will follow her wherever she goes, even if it means I have to work out. I wanted to be one of those pregnant "fit" moms, but I couldn't walk around my neighborhood because I didn't want paparazzi photos of me huffing and puffing, so the treadmill seemed like a good fix. At first I *was* one of those fit moms. I walked two miles almost every day, until I couldn't take it anymore, which was pretty much at the end of my second trimester, when every joint began to ache and I began to waddle from side to side like my late grandmother. Once I stopped, my workouts consisted of raising my heart rate by scooping ice cream out of the container. I got back on the NordicTrack again after Hartford was born to try to achieve my pre-baby weight, like Jessica. Funny thing is, the weight doesn't just "fall off" after pregnancy, like some women say. Breastfeeding doesn't turn you into a supermodel. And so, I walked.

The NordicTrack was great because, similar to my VR sets, you could travel! Mine came with these big TV screens, and I could scroll through different videos in different countries so I felt like I was hiking or walking through a whole new city. I spent my whole 2020 summer walking through German Christmas markets. (I told you I love Christmas.) I was able to channel my love of *Outlander* into my workouts by hiking through the Scottish Highlands with one of the cast members as my guide. I could also take a brisk walk through London while a tour guide taught me all about the serial killers who lived there. Highly recommend them all.

Even though I still missed business and work, self-care became more important to me than ever as my pregnancy went on, because the closer I got to my due date, the more terrified I became of postpartum depression. I felt like all the environmental factors were lined up accordingly to add up to postpartum depression for me. If having a baby and having your hormones go all whack wasn't enough, then I factored in that I was stuck at home due to a worldwide disease, and I had been fired from all the jobs that made me happy, and that my body was approximately 23,498,723 pounds heavier than it had ever been. How could I not get postpartum depression?! Since I was a first-time mom, I had no idea what to expect, so I didn't even know how to plan for whatever self-care I would need after the baby was born. I wasn't convinced that strapping on a VR headset and taking murder tours of London would help.

I think what I've learned the most is that self-care truly is doing what you need to be happy as a means of survival, especially during a dark time like Covid or if you've lost a job or have gone through incredibly rough times. Doing things to keep myself happy during a rock-bottom time became incredibly important. Even the way I started my day became a part of my survival self-care routine. I began by making mornings fun, or trying to. I'd wake up as late as my body would allow me to, Beau would bring me an iced coffee, I'd open my windows, light a holiday candle even if it was July, and spend a good hour and a half just chilling in bed, and scrolling through things on my phone that interested me. I knew that once I had my baby, those days would be long gone, so starting each morning like that was my way of taking advantage of being jobless during a pandemic. If I was going to have all this time on my hands, then I should at least try to enjoy it, because it wasn't going to be that way forever.

I also turned my nightly routine into a self-care ritual. At around 8:00 p.m. I'd soak in a long bath, and really take my time getting ready for bed. I installed a TV in the bedroom, which is something neither Beau nor I had ever done. One reason is that too much stimulation makes it hard for me to sleep, another is that I wanted to associate my bedroom with romance and relaxation, and yet another is that getting food on the bed while you watch TV is gross. But I figured, I'm pregnant, I'm going to want to lie down in bed a little more than usual, and since I can't travel, I may as well make my bedroom a little like a hotel room. So we put in a TV and started using the wet bar in our hallway to feel like we were on vacay. We could just walk into the hallway and grab a water or an iced coffee or a cucumber face mist—all sober luxury items. I would also make Beau give me a back rub while we watched movies together, which is supes romantic to me. Things like that kept me sane and in a good mood, and self-care is all about keeping yourself in a good mood, especially when you're at rock bottom.

Before Hartford came along, I had no idea what self-care would look like with a tiny human to feed and clothe and burp and whatever else I thought you did to keep babies happy. During pregnancy, if I had to hear one more person tell me, "Enjoy sleep while you can!" I was going to rip my hair out. Once Hartford came along and once the early newborn days and nights of *What the hell do we do with this tiny baby?* were over and we settled into this parenting thing, my self-care routine only happened at night after seven thirty, when I'd officially put her down for bed. As I write this, she goes to bed at seven thirty! We'll see if that lasts. . . . Anyway, after 7:30 p.m., like a reverse Cinderella, I feel like the world is my oyster, like anything is possible (within the walls of my own home, obvs). I need to get better at making more "couple time" for me and Beau, but for the first several months at least, it's been ME TIME. That "me time" consists of deciding whether I want to go straight to bed or stay awake and do things that might rejuvenate me, like drinking wine while watching *Keeping Up With the Kardashians* reruns and scrolling through TikTok. Basically, those precious hours at night are the only "me time" I'm getting now, and I cherish every glorious moment. I've been so happy since Hartford was born, and since I thought for sure I was going to have postpartum depression, I feel lucky that I didn't get it. It was a rough year, and I don't think I would have been able to handle that.

Stassi's Rock-Bottom Self-Care Tips

Take a staycation: Sometimes you need to check the eff out and get away, but maybe you don't have the time or the energy or the funds to actually plan a trip that involves travel. After weeks of nonstop filming, we were exhausted (even though we always had a blast). So instead of sitting on the couch in sweats, we decided to just take a staycation. We got a hotel room by the beach in Santa Monica, packed up our dogs, and just went to dinner and walked on the sand. It's a good way to feel like you're getting away, even though you might only be fifteen miles from your couch.

Mute the world: As you may remember from reading *Next Level Basic*, I would never advocate for letting your phone run out of charge, or even getting below 60 percent. But I do advocate for putting that sucker on mute when you need to truly relax. I'm talking no Instagram, no Facebook, no news alerts (even if they are about Meghan Markle). I know I'm missing out on certain things when I do this, but if I really need "me time," my heart drops when I hear the ding of my phone. Just mute it, turn it over, and focus on watching *Bridgerton* (or reading a book). Do it for your health.

Guests be gone: Is there anything worse than someone overstaying their welcome at your house? It's so hard to tell people to leave without sounding like a jerk, but don't be a pushover when it comes to this—they'll get over it. Just politely tell them that you need to not speak for a little bit. People who overstay their welcome really bother me. Can't you read a room? Can't you understand the energy that's swirling around, whispering, *BYE, FELICIA, GTFO of my house?* Just remember that they won't die if you ask them to go, and the payoff will be you, alone, on the couch with your dogs and TV. It's always a win.

Treat yourself: When I get overwhelmed and I realize that I still have a long day ahead of me, I think of some way that I'm going to treat myself later on that day or night. It could be ordering dinner from a fancy restaurant, allowing myself to online shop and buy some bejeweled shoes, or just taking the last hour before bed to take a hot shower and read an Anne Boleyn biography in bed. Keep in mind that was my way of treating myself pre-baby and pre-Covid. Your version of treating yourself might be giving yourself a pedicure or buying yourself some nice flowers for no reason (other than that you're a badass).

Rock-Bottom TAKEAWAY

Is there such a thing as too much self-care? Maybe. But that doesn't mean you shouldn't confine your pampering to "Self-Care Sundays." If you're down, whether from a fight with a friend or a lost job or just someone being annoying at the grocery store, you deserve to do whatever it is that makes *you* feel relaxed and happy AF. A bubble bath, a video game binge, VR exploration of Morocco . . . find your self-care routine and don't ever feel guilty for indulging. Even with a baby, it's okay to take a little time to steam your face or have some cucumber water and play "Jingle Bells." Self-care is vital, and it's important to find the little rituals that work for you so you can turn to them when you're feeling crappy. Highly recommend.

· CHAPTER 11 ·

Basic Baby

You cannot get more basic bitch than a gender-reveal party. You know the parties where people invite their friends and family over to find out the sex of their unborn child by cutting into a cake that's either pink or blue inside, because no other colors could possibly signify male or female? Or maybe instead of a cake, they launch a rocket full of pink or blue confetti or set off cannons filled with blue or pink smoke. They're ridiculous, and I freaking love them.

Real talk: before I became pregnant, Katie and I used to send each other screenshots of people's ridiculous gender-reveal party posts and make fun of them. There are psycho people out there who have gender-reveal parties that are bigger and more extravagant than most weddings. I just can't with those. They have step-and-repeat banners for red carpet–like photo ops (WTF!), sponsored dessert bars, fireworks, and magicians. I have seen gender-reveal parties with more than one hundred people there. Like, do one hundred people actually care what gender your baby is? Probably not. Let's not fool ourselves. I still have major opinions about over-the-top gender-reveal parties, but I will say, once I became pregnant, I realized just how meaningful they can be. I was almost as excited during Lala's and Brittany's gender reveals as I was for my own.

In the BC (Before Cancellation) times, Beau and I were absolutely dead-set on hiring one of those little planes to fly around Hollywood and Valley Village with a banner trailing after it that read, "It's a boy!" or "It's a girl!" We were a few months into the pandemic when I got pregnant, so an actual party wasn't reasonable. We figured that our friends and family could just walk outside their respective houses and see the plane, and we could all celebrate. Then the After Cancellation era descended on our lives like a tsunami, and I was in no mood to make a big show of my pregnancy. I didn't want to have a gender reveal at all at that point, but Beau was adamant about it. He was not about to let my canceling take away from this moment, and I'm so appreciative he pushed for it. What else did I have to look forward to in the spring or summer of 2020 besides baked goods and doom-scrolling on Twitter? There was so little to celebrate in 2020 that I'm glad I didn't miss this opportunity.

We decided to have my mom and siblings and a few of our friends come over for a very socially distanced reveal. My sister is one of the most talented bakers I know, so I had my doctor call her with the gender, and she made me the most beautiful cake that had a vintage Victorian vibe. My sister describes it as "a berry Gentilly Southern cake with Victorian and art nouveau elements."

I describe it as "round with white icing and cute lace detail." The cake read "The Clark Passenger" as a nod to my psycho alter-ego, the Dark Passenger, from the serial killer show *Dexter*. That day will go down as one of the best days of my life. That's when it clicked, when I found out it was a girl. You're one step closer to knowing who is inside your belly, and in that moment I totally understood why gender-reveal parties are a thing. The night before the reveal, I couldn't sleep. It felt like the night before Christmas. I don't know if I could ever properly explain the total elation and joy I felt when we cut into the cake and saw pink. I didn't realize how much I wanted a girl until that moment. She suddenly became so much more real to me. So while, yes, I still judge over-the-top gender reveals, I do get it now. I think gender reveals are really for the people who will be around the child the most, like the parents, the family, and your closest friends. No one else gives a shit about whether your baby is born a boy or girl. Even though I went full basic bitch and had one, I still very much understand people who are opposed to gender reveals. Besides the fact that they can be dangerous and actually start statewide fires or kill your guests if you use a pyrotechnic device, I understand that too much emphasis on gender can be alienating and hurtful. You never know how your child is going to identify. We wanted to celebrate the journey we were on at that moment, and if our daughter one day decides to take the brave step of declaring that they're nonbinary or gender-queer or anything else, we'll support them 100 percent. Until then, I reserve the right to dress her like a monochromatic, elegant tiny Parisian princess and have a gender-reveal party.

Having a gender reveal wasn't the only basic thing I did during pregnancy. I also freaked out about my body changing, instead of being one of those earth mothers who embrace all their new "curves" and rolls and bulges. I truly had no idea that my body would feel like it was suddenly ninety-three years old, that it would ache to walk around too much, that my knees would buckle at times, that my joints would hurt whenever I tried to sit down or that my back would have shooting pains if I sat or laid down in the wrong position for too long. Don't even get me started on the once simple act of bending down to pick something up. You see pregnant women waddling around all the time and holding their backs as if they're in pain, but pregnancy seriously *hurts*, and it's not cute like it is in movies. I didn't look adorable like Katherine Heigl in *Knocked Up*. I felt like a whale that swallowed a walrus that had just eaten a large pig. And maybe the pig had eaten fifteen tons of Krispy Kreme.

I actually didn't realize how self-conscious I would be through-out pregnancy. I thought that I would totally embrace any change that happened to my body and just celebrate it as a part of my journey, but hard no on that. There were many days full of self-loathing, days I spent comparing myself to other women who were pregnant at the same time I was, like Emma Roberts or Gigi Hadid. Pro tip, I definitely do not recommend being pregnant at the same time as Emily Ratajkowski in her crop tops and silk slip dresses. I guess I knew things would balloon a little here and there, but I never expected my actual body type to change. There is so much emphasis on women's pregnant bodies in the media. People want to pick apart every pound a woman gains. I read so many comments on social media whenever I posted pregnant photos, and it felt like everyone had an opinion about my pregnant body. People said I looked like I was showing too soon ("she's only five months; she looks nine months!"), or that I was huge, a Goodyear blimp with a ponytail and legs. There were also nice comments, people saying that I was glowing and gorgeous, but that's not what I saw when I looked in the mirror. My changing looks made me so self-conscious I barely wanted to go anywhere. I hate saying that, but it's true. I thought I would be a really confident pregnant woman, but that unfortunately wasn't the case. I would love to say I felt like some sort of modern-day fertility goddess, but I'm just being real. I felt like a blob in sweatpants most of the time. Worrying about my baby's health was by far the most stressful part of pregnancy. It makes all the stress about weight or swollen feet seem like nothing. At one of my ultrasound appointments the doctor saw a hole in the baby's heart, and waiting to hear back about what that could mean was by far the worst week of my life. I would have taken being canceled on repeat every day for the rest of my life over living that week again. It ended up being a common issue that thankfully resolved itself, but I know so many parents go through these scares, and they are brutal.

I wish more people talked about the gross or tough or not-so-cute side of pregnancy. Like the hemorrhoids. They were the absolute worst. I could hardly sit down at times. This is me telling you I had swollen veins in my rectum and hoping you still keep reading! There's also the constant gas, the restless leg syndrome, the stuffy nose that turned me into a mouth breather and a monster snorer (Beau sometimes slept on the couch), the swollen ankles and feet, and the discharge. So. Much. Discharge. If that's TMI, too bad. You try being pregnant without having your bodily functions turn you into a walking, talking, oozing sea monster.

Besides the fact that I felt huge and uncomfortable and had a swollen butt most days, one pleasant surprise with pregnancy was that it made me feel incredibly powerful. I don't mean that it made me feel gorgeous, but most of the time I felt like some sort of superwoman. In case you're wondering, a woman *can* feel insecure AF and *also* feel like an all-powerful hero. There is nothing like pregnancy to make you realize how incredibly strong women are. Men could never handle this shit. Beau whines 24-7 if he has a sniffle. Women handle so much every single day, all while taking care of business in every way possible—multitasking, working, feeding the kids, often at the same time. Being canceled while being pregnant and not losing my mind made me feel like I could literally do anything or handle anything. Yes, I broke down crying a lot, but when I was finished I took a bath, put on some lipstick and a new pair of sweatpants, and ate a damn cupcake, like a boss!

Stassi's Pregnancy Food Pyramid

"HEALTHY" DESSERTS

LOOK! FRUIT!

WAFFLES ALL DAY LONG

ANOTHER DONUT

DONUT

COOKIES AND BROWNIES

ALL. THE. CAKE.

Breakfast desserts: Eggos, Belgian waffles, pancakes, cinnamon rolls, maple and brown sugar oatmeal, apple cinnamon oatmeal, doughnuts, strawberry shortcake biscuits, blueberry muffins

Regular desserts: Funfetti cake, chocolate chip cookies, Phish Food ice cream, double-chocolate-chunk brownies, any flavor of cake, apple pie, cherry pie, (pasteurized) cookie dough, cheesecake, crème brûlée, panna cotta, molten lava cakes, tres leches . . .

Desserts I told myself were healthy: Strawberries and cream, raspberries and chocolate

Candy: Sour Patch Kids (red and blue flavors), Reese's, Ghirardelli milk chocolate and caramel squares, Godiva truffles

* Fun fact! I didn't crave Ranch even once during my pregnancy. It's not like I gave it up completely though, I obviously still ate it with my pizza and salads, but it was just not on my radar at all.

That said, I had a pretty easy pregnancy, which makes it unfair to talk like I'm some maternal sorceress. I never got sick or threw up, and in terms of being hormonal and emotional, well, I'm already like that normally, so it wasn't a huge shift. The worst part of pregnancy for me, besides being terrified about a supposed hole in my baby's heart obviously, was the weight gain, but that's my fault. I totally didn't deprive myself, and I allowed myself to just chill out and enjoy that pregnant quarantine life as much as I could. The amount of sugar I consumed was disconcerting, and I was shocked when I passed my gestational diabetes test. Naturally I celebrated my A+ grade with ice cream. The last month did kick my ass though, and no amount of ice cream could cure my aches and pains. (Well, depending on the flavor.) At the end I just felt like, "I'm good—can I tap out now?" I really wanted to call it quits, because nine months feels like one month too long.

The thing is, you're just so tired all the time. Like ridiculously tired. A kind of tired I've never felt before. Yet when it was time for bed, it was impossible to get to sleep because I was so uncomfortable or I was waking up every thirty minutes to pee. WHY?! I also transformed into an eighty-three-year-old burly man who grunts his way through any movement. Truly, I couldn't get out of a chair without grunting. I couldn't unload the dishwasher without grunting. I could barely change the channel on my remote without grunting. ACTUAL GRUNTS. There's no way Beau can still be attracted to me after that. During the last month, my brain just stopped working. Even as I type this, I'm not sure I'm making any sense. I'll have a thought, and then if I get distracted for even half a second, that thought is long gone, never to be thought of again. . . .

Here's a thought: pregnancy is HARD AF!

I realize I may sound like a vapid superficial broken record, but the amount of breakdowns I had over my changing body knew no end. My closet is painted with the tears of my pregnant swollen face. I would sob to Beau and make him promise me that we would throw away all the Sour Patch Kids (that never happened) and that he wouldn't let me eat dessert anymore (he didn't dare try to follow through with that one either). There is so much pressure on women to love their pregnant bodies because we're creating life, but it's freaking difficult. Yes, I felt so lucky to be pregnant, and yes, it's incredible what our bodies can do, but I'm also still allowed to freak out and mourn the loss of my former self. It doesn't mean I love my baby any less. It just means I'd love my baby more if I hadn't gotten all this back fat. KIDDING. There is actual footage of me on my mom's boat in Lake Arrowhead, where I'm cursing and trying to fight the camera out of Beau's hands because I didn't want him recording me or my triple chin. It was Dark Passenger to the nth degree.

I don't think I was properly warned enough for my first post-baby sex experience, or for post-baby sex at all for that matter. I mean, an entire human being has been shoved out the same hole that my husband's you-know-what is supposed to go in—for plea-sure?! It's been torn open and stitched up, which is just as psy-chologically damaging as it is physically. And don't get me started on my new postpartum body and deflated tummy (well, I already started, but you get it). Throw in the crazy hormonal changes and you get a recipe for the least horny woman alive. The last thing on my mind after giving birth was sexy time. Women are advised to wait until their six-week postpartum doctor's appointment so that the doctor can give you the okay to exercise and have sex. I remember being at that appointment and getting chills when my doctor said I was perfectly fine to be intimate again. I half joked that I wasn't ready, and he told me that many women who have come before me have asked him to write a doctor's note for their husbands to say that those women weren't ready yet. I guess most women are just as scared shitless as I was.

Taking my first postpartum poop was one of the more horrific moments of my life, so how was I going to be able to handle sex? Despite my terror, I declined the doctor's note and told Beau I was in the clear. I also told him I was going to require four spicy mar-garitas beforehand, and that I was going to wear a girdle around my tummy, or no deal. It probably didn't help that my vagina closed up and felt tight throughout my whole pregnancy. If it hurt when I was pregnant, then it was absolutely going to hurt after getting stitches, or so I thought. But to my surprise, our first time back was one of the best sexy times we'd had in ages. We put the baby down to bed, I dimmed the lights, put on my little waist-cincher thing, had some tequila, and it worked! It didn't hurt whatsoever. I guess my baby stretched out the tightness? Joking. But maybe I'm not. Either way, when we were all done, we literally did victory dances and high-fived a million times. But I will say it was way harder for me to get in the mood after having a baby. I wasn't comfortable in my body, I was exhausted by the end of the day from taking care of Hartford, I still felt like my hormones are out of sorts, and the fact that Beau and I had been quarantined in the house together for a year when the majority of our relationship was spent traveling and having fun didn't exactly help to ignite spontaneous passion. We had to make intimacy time a priority. It's been something that we talk about regularly and that we make sure to schedule in (I know that doesn't sound romantic, but we have a baby, so we have to). I think there is something romantic about the fact that we are both so willing to talk about it and make it a priority for each other. I'm hoping one of these days I'll feel back to my old spontaneous sexy self, but for now I take it one day at a time.

One thing that helped during pregnancy and postpartum was going through all of this at the same time as some of my closest friends. I remember all of us always joking about how we wanted to get pregnant at the same time, but Lala had to remind me that we did actually make a pregnancy pact. It happened in 2018 when we were all on a private jet heading to Cabo for Lala's birthday. I sound like such a braggy douche, but facts are facts. I didn't remember the actual sacred pact because I was hammered and that was the trip that made me realize I had to quit Adderall for good. Lala says that we shook hands along with Brittany and Katie and vowed that when the first one of us got pregnant, the others would try as well. Did we, like, do a magic spell or cut our hands and put them together in a blood oath? No. But there had to have been some sort of witchcraft going on because Lala and Brittany got pregnant three months after I did.

As funny as a pregnancy pact may be, I've felt a little uncomfortable talking about it, because getting pregnant is not that easy, and I don't want to make it sound like it is. Yes, we had a pregnancy pact, but it's dangerous to act like anyone can just get pregnant at the snap of a finger. It hasn't been that easy for all of us. Brittany had been trying for a while before she got pregnant, and she was even worried that she might need to see a fertility specialist. Katie has been trying, but it hasn't happened yet. Brittany, Lala, and I got very lucky, and we're each very much aware of that. It's truly one of the greatest gifts to go through pregnancy with other pregnant friends. I remember right when I found out I was pregnant, it was one of the only times I had ever experienced FOMO. I immediately freaked out that my friends would never have me around anymore, that they'd continue to go on girls' trips without me, that Beau and I wouldn't be included in any of the group activities anymore. What a relief it was when two more friends became pregnant! We'd all be growing up together. We'd all be able to relate to what we were each going through. It was such a damn blessing to go through this with my friends. I could complain to them about anything, and they'd get it. We had each other to rely on for advice. Best of all, our kids get to grow up together. To say it's special would be a massive understatement.

We created a group chat where we were constantly updating each other, complaining, or asking for advice. Lala always told me she was thankful I was going first so I could teach her all the things. Ha! Each of our pregnancy journeys were so different. Brittany was sick her entire pregnancy, throwing up multiple times a day and unable to leave her house. Yet she still always talks about how she loved pregnancy and can't wait to get pregnant again. Lala was in the hospital a lot in the beginning of her pregnancy because she had early complications. And while I wasn't sick and thankfully didn't have any complications, I had to go through finding out my daughter had a hole in her heart. Brittany thought her belly showed too much, and Lala got insecure that hers didn't show enough. Lala had a hotter pregnant body than I did when I was at my peak prepregnancy hottest. She loved posting naked photos, and looked damn good in them. I, on the other hand, hung around in sweatpants all day long. Brittany and I started our nurseries immediately after discovering we were pregnant, while Lala waited until the last minute. It was totes different for all of us. But going through it together was seriously comforting AF.

My absolute favorite part of pregnancy was feeling the baby move around like she was straight out of the movie *Alien* when the extraterrestrial being starts writhing around in that poor guy's stomach. It's so gross when you really think about it, but it's also so freaking magical. I didn't care that she kept me up at night by kicking me in the ribs because I loved it so much. It also made me feel like I was hanging out with a friend when I was by myself. I totally get the fact that that sounds psychotic, but technically it's true.

On the other side, one of the worst things about pregnancy (besides weight gain, hemorrhoids, and excruciating pain) is the next-level swelling. My swelling started to happen very early on, like during my eighteenth week. I looked like Kim Kardashian when she was pregnant and bubbling out of her strappy heels. My swelling was so bad that my mom thought I was going to have major pregnancy complications and be put on bed rest. Yes, the swelling was fugly and painful, but what hurt the most was the fact that I couldn't wear any of my shoes. My shoe closet is one of my most prized collections. I have spent my whole life collecting shoes, because no matter what happens with weight gain or fluctuations or your mood, you can always rely on your shoes to fit and make you feel pretty. Pregnancy stole that from me. I'm normally a shoe size 7.5, and I was wearing a size 9 during my pregnancy. Some people told me that my feet would go back to normal, and others told me that their feet never deflated after pregnancy. Do you know how many sparkly bedazzled shoes I've collected over the years?! They *have* to go back down. Four months after giving birth, I fit into only half of my shoes. Wasn't being canceled enough of a heartache to go through in 2020? Did my shoes really have to be taken away from me too?

When I wasn't weeping in my shoe closet or devouring Sour Patch Kids by the fistful (or both at the same time), I read baby books. The second I became pregnant, Beau bought 98,734 pregnancy books for us. I have a love/hate relationship with pregnancy books. I either loved the book or hated it, there was no in between. I found that I really liked books that were relatable and not so serious. Yes, your standard *What to Expect When You're Expecting (WTEWYE)* is helpful AF, but it's not exactly a fun read. I used *WTEWYE* as a kind of dictionary. Whenever I had a question about something pregnancy related, I'd look it up there. Unfortunately there were no chapters about how to handle grieving your unwearable prepregnancy shoes. Note to the editors of that book: the next addition totes needs that chapter. It'll help millions of women.

I absolutely loved *Expecting Better* by Emily Oster. This bitch knows what's up. She's an economist who used actual data and research to debunk so many common pregnancy rules. Once you become pregnant, it seems like everything becomes off-limits. Wine, deli meat, sushi, tuna, caffeine, a million cheeses, dying your hair, hot baths, many medications. I even read lists that said not to wear stilettos! Tell that to Meghan Markle and Beyoncé. Before I read *Expecting Better*, it seemed like pregnancy was just one long list of "don't do this" and "don't eat that," and that is seriously a *bore*. With a lot of research, Emily Oster shows us that so many of those things on the "don't" list can actually be had in moderation. You can have sushi once in a while, just don't eat sushi from a gas station or a state fair in the Midwest. You can have a coffee, just don't drink a million Red Bulls. I was not into those strict pregnancy rules, so this book was right up my alley.

My other fave was *The Girlfriend's Guide to Pregnancy* by Vicki Iovine. Basically this book was what I would imagine my book would be like if I wrote a whole book about pregnancy. It's relatable AF. I really felt like she was my friend, just shooting the shit about what to expect on your pregnancy journey. It didn't make me feel pressured to get everything right; it left me feeling like every thought or feeling I had was normal. Highly recommended. I'm not going to name the books I could do without, because that's just rude. I will say, if the book had namaste vibes, or if it made the whole pregnancy thing sound too serious or earth mother–y, I just had to toss it aside. Yes, pregnancy is serious, but like, women have been doing it since the beginning of time, so if I don't master the one-minute breath-mindfulness exercise or write a three-and-a-half-page birth plan, I'm pretty sure my baby and I are still going to be fine. I can be very type A in most areas of my life, but somehow pregnancy was not one of those areas. Besides sobbing about weight gain and swollen feet, I was a chill, cool-girl pregnant chick. SMH. Who the hell *was* I for those nine months?!

As for Beau, he actually read some "just for dads" pregnancy books, and he had major opinions about them. His main complaint was: "All the books are for bro-type dads. I'm not a bro-dad. I don't need to be taught to embrace pink if I'm having a girl, because I already like pink. I'm a creative artsy type." I'm paraphrasing, but that's pretty much what he said. I think Beau liked the pregnancy books geared toward women more than the ones for fathers. I will say this, I noticed that he started off strong with the books, and then gave it up after a month. It wasn't until the last month that he started doing all of his research again. I didn't want to be naggy and hound him to keep up the reading throughout my pregnancy, so I just left it alone and continued to educate myself. But once I got into the last month of my pregnancy, it became very real to him, and it lit a fire under his booty. Like, *Oh shit, this baby isn't just this intangible thing that's going to appear sometime in the distant future. This baby is going to be here any minute, so I better do some reading!* I wonder if it's like this for most men. It's so real to the women throughout the process because we're watching and feeling our bellies grow every day, but for men, it's not as obvious or tangible. Or maybe men are just slower in general? In any case, I'm thankful that Beau read some books.

Some of the books were helpful, but there is such a thing as TMA—too much advice. I've never received more random texts and DMs from people giving advice on any other topic as I did with pregnancy. It actually never annoyed me. I welcomed all advice. Did I take it? Not always, but I liked hearing about other people's perspectives and experiences. I, too, caught myself giving unsolicited advice. I cringed one time I dished it out, because I felt like such a Karen, because it was over something so dumb. I was at dinner with Brittany one night, and I noticed in her Instagram Stories earlier that day that she had a venti Starbucks Frappuccino, and then at dinner she was ordering a million sweet teas. So I said something along the lines of "You know, Brittany, you really need to watch your caffeine intake, especially since you're not out of your first trimester yet." What a judgy asscrack. Why did I feel the need to say that? Was it just a rite of passage to pass on some hyper-critical, annoying, unsolicited advice at least once? Was I doing that annoying *I became pregnant first, so I know things* BS? I still look back on that and get the cringe sweats because I could tell I made her feel bad. It was her body and her pregnancy. She's an adult. Who was I to have an opinion and say it out loud? Total dick move. Lesson learned though. I never dished out judgy advice again.

Besides my books, I think the best advice I got was from my college roommate Niki. She had her first baby within the first few months of quarantine, and thank the Lord for her. It truly is the greatest gift to have friends going through the same thing. It was so helpful that she had just gone through pregnancy and then labor, because everything was still fresh in her mind. Something very simple that she said really made me feel so much more at ease. She said, "The last month can feel so slow because you're so ready and over being pregnant. Just try to relax and rest, because it'll be a whirlwind when she gets here. Chill and do nothing and watch TV and be unproductive." I think it was so nice to get some sort of permission or confirmation that it was fine to just rest. All I wanted to do was sit in my pregnancy pillow, watch holiday baking shows, and scroll through TikTok. It was exhausting to even lift my arms and hands to type or send an email. Her advice will be my advice to my friends. Our bodies have been through a lot over nine months, we *should* be resting and being unproductive when we need to be, because our bodies are doing the most productive thing they possibly can. So let's give ourselves grace to just chill, and drink some sweet teas if we want to.

The worst advice I got came from strangers who had opinions

about *everything*: I should get rid of the canopy over my daughter's crib because she would rip it down and it would suffocate her. I should get rid of the OOTD mirror in her room because it'll crush her. I should never have bought so many baby clothes because she'll never wear them. Thank you, Brenda, but I didn't ask for your opinion!

I thank my lucky stars that I married someone who did not judge me during pregnancy and who cooks for me every day. I totes don't ever take that for granted. As a pregnant person, all I wanted was to be fed. Okay, that's not all I wanted. I also wanted massages, back rubs, foot rubs, for Beau to take over all the chores, and for him to have the patience and sympathy to allow me to emotionally break down over something as lame as spilling my cereal. I want to shout out all the single mamas out there, the ones who do this pregnancy thing on their own. They are true queens. Their strength and resilience is incredible, and they deserve *all* the respect.

But back to me. I'm starting to think I didn't use the pregnancy thing to my advantage enough. I think I acted too unfazed by my pregnancy symptoms at times in an effort to seem chill or strong, and I missed my window of opportunity to truly milk that shit. I milked it plenty, but maybe I could have done more?

Up until the final month, I think Beau thought I was an actual superhero. Like I've said, my worst symptoms were constipation and annoying weight gain that led to multiple chins, but those are hardly things that deserve extra special attention. I rarely complained, which is completely not my nature. Normally I absolutely would classify myself as a complainer. I love complaining! I think it's fun. I don't know what I was thinking when I spent the first eight months acting like *I got this*. Once I got to the final month, when I could barely move and everything ached, Beau was so used to me still taking care of myself that I think it came as a shock that I needed help with literally everything. Help picking up something I dropped on the floor, help with my wacko hormonal mood swings, help rolling over, help buying more baked goods. You get the picture. Why did I wait until the last month to ask for help?!

There is so much pressure to be the perfect pregnant chick who has it all together, but why? This is our only time to truly take advantage of our situation and be waited on hand and foot. I'm so disappointed in myself for playing the cool pregnant chick at times. The cool pregnant chick is way overrated. Next time around (which I hope will not be any time in the next few years so I can enjoy Hartford and get my life back together), I'm going to act like a broken doll for nine months straight. I don't want to sound ungrateful for the support Beau gave me. I'm supes appreciative he took over all the dog chores. He was always asking me if I needed anything, he brought my coffee to the bedroom every morning, he hugged me instead of getting angry every time I had an emotional meltdown and attacked him for something, and he gave me a massage every time I asked. But . . . I still feel like I could've gotten some more out of him. I should have milked it to the point where I didn't have to ask for massages, he'd just offer them! So, ladies, my advice to you is to reject the cool pregnant girl stereotype and TAKE ADVANTAGE of the fact that you are literally growing a freaking alien baby inside of you and sacrificing your body and sanity to bring a child into this world. Someone needs to learn from my mistakes, and I hope it's you.

You can read every single book out there about pregnancy, but the bottom line is that everyone's experience is different, so if Flamin' Hot Cheetos and twenty-six naps a day are what you need to feel like your best self, then do it. As tough as pregnancy can be, it gave me a whole new perspective on what's important, and it made things that would normally send me spiraling seem manageable because I had a tiny human to take care of. It's painful trying to squeeze your swollen size 9 feet into your old size 7.5 heels (literally and figuratively), but you will get through it. If you're having a bad day where all you can see are your back-fat bulges and your butt is sore from hemorrhoids, take care of yourself and remember that you are a freaking superwoman, even if you're wearing sweatpants stained with cake batter.

Best and Worst Pregnancy Purchases

Just like advice, you're bombarded with ads for a lot of things you ABSOLUTELY NEED TO BUY when you're pregnant and expecting a baby. The thing is, you only need like two of them. Like I said before, women have been birthing babies for centuries, and last I checked they didn't have maternity shapewear and compression socks in the Middle Ages or the cavewoman days. It took me a while to figure out what was worth buying and what I wished I'd kept the receipt for. Here are the best and worst things I bought during my nine months of carrying a baby around.

The Best

Pregnancy pillows: I could not have survived without my pregnancy pillows. Yes, that's *pillows*, plural. I had multiple pregnancy pillows because I didn't have the energy to lug one up and down the stairs, and obviously I couldn't rest on the couch or bed without one of these six-foot-long, unwieldy things that look like a gigantic, comfy snake. I think Beau resented the pillows. He said they created a barrier between us, and they made him forget what it was like to cuddle. He claimed that he would wake up at night cuddling what he thought was my cushy preggo body, only to discover he was spooning the pillow. You know what? He got over it, and I *needed* that pillow. It helps you get comfortable, relieves back pain or leg cramps, and lets you sleep when you have a giant bump protruding from your stomach. How did Neanderthal women go through pregnancy without these?!

Unisom: I've been open about my past reliance on Xanax. I've had sleeping problems for the past fifteen years of my life and have always relied on medication. It's not healthy or okay, but I'm trying to be honest here. When I found out I was pregnant, I obviously knew the Xanax part of my life was over. My doctor said Unisom, an over-the-counter sleeping aid, was 100 percent safe to take while pregnant, so I ordered them in bulk. If I hadn't had Unisom, I would've truly lost my mind. Throughout my pregnancy, I often thought of all the women who were pregnant before 1978, the year Unisom was created. HOW DID PREGNANT WOMEN GET TO SLEEP WITHOUT IT? If you say "chamomile tea" I will burst into literal flames.

Squatty Potty: An absolutely necessary purchase that I swore I would never buy because I thought they looked geriatric and weird. Eventually I caved, and I found a wooden one, which I found a tad more aesthetically pleasing than the all-white version. It's not sexy, but it was a huge help with pregnancy constipation.

UGG slippers: Like I mentioned, none of my shoes fit and I was quarantined in my house, so I rotated UGG slippers all day, every day. I used to wear cute, girly furry-chic slippers around the house, and suddenly I looked down and my shoes looked like they belonged to an eighty-three-year-old lunch lady, but a stylish lunch lady who wears UGGs, I guess.

Cashmere sweat sets: These saved me when my body shape was going through all the changes. I was pear-shaped throughout my pregnancy, but prepregnancy, I was the opposite. I was always big on top and tiny on the bottom, like a damn lollipop. Most of my baby weight went to my thighs and butt, and since I had no experience with this body type, I had no clue how to dress it. Matching cashmere sweats kept me super comfy. They were roomy, but they also made me feel somewhat chic. My favorites were from HATCH.

Black long-sleeved body-con dresses: Pretty much the only look I wore the few times I actually left the house. Pregnancy dressing is hard, y'all.

Shower mirror: I bought this so I could shave down there without butchering myself. After week twenty of pregnancy, I couldn't see my vagina, so this was supes necessary. I asked Beau for help shaving down there, and he got too scared and chickened out. Men. Why do women have to do everything?!

Pregnancy ball: Chairs, couches, hammocks, bean bags, pool floats, and beds became uncomfortable during pregnancy. The bouncy ball I got was the only place I could sit without getting a pain somewhere.

The Worst

Maternity shapewear: I bought so much shapewear in the beginning of my pregnancy because I wasn't used to my body getting lumpier by the minute and I thought it might help smooth and flatten and smash down some of the parts I didn't like. Honestly, though, the last thing I wanted while I was pregnant was to restrict myself with shapewear. It's much more comfortable to just let it all hang out. Now I have a drawer of unused maternity shapewear, if any of you pregnant bitches want to torture yourself.

Nonalcoholic wine: I missed everything about wine during my pregnancy. The sound of the cork pop, the smell, the taste, swishing it around in a wineglass, the feeling of being shit-faced. Kidding about that last one. Okay, maybe I'm not. I found a nonalcoholic wine that had a million stars on Amazon, so I ordered a bunch. That delivery was a real buzzkill. Not only does it just not taste the same (think very tangy grape juice), but what's the point if you're not getting a little buzz? Why waste the calories on that when you have baked goods to devour? Do not recommend.

Going-out maternity clothes: I have a closet full of unused fancy maternity dresses and jumpsuits, and it's too late to return any of it. It puts me in an absolutely horrible mood every time I think about it. WHY DID I DO THIS? Did I not realize that I was pregnant during a worldwide pandemic and that I wouldn't be able to leave my house? Where did I think I was going to be wearing all these clothes? All I needed were my sweats, my UGG slippers, a bodycon dress or two, and a large cardigan to throw over the dress, and I was set. Maybe if I had been going to an office every day or waddling around to meetings I would have worn some of the things I bought, but that didn't happen. I know it's not a massive problem in the whole scheme of life, but still. What a waste!

Stassi's Guide to Baby OOTDs

Is there anything cuter than freaking baby clothes?! The answer to that is an obvious *no*, there's not. I took my daughter's wardrobe so seriously that I pretty much sent out an announcement warning friends and family that I would not be accepting baby clothes as gifts. My mom, my sister, and my best friends all knew not to buy her a single piece of clothing unless they ran it by me first. I had a very clear vision for what I wanted her wardrobe to consist of, and I just didn't want anyone to go wasting their money on bright pink onesies, giant bows, or sequined bloomers. My baby is chic. She's into neutrals, she's not overly girly, and she loves a monochromatic look. I totally get that I sound crazy, and I'm totally okay with it. Isn't it, like, a rite of passage for first-time moms to treat their firstborns like dolls?

I bought her entire first-year wardrobe by the midway mark of my pregnancy, and everything was washed, hung up, and ready by my third trimester. She has about thirty pairs of shoes, and before any mom shamers lay into me, I very much understand she will only be wearing them for photos. I just can't wait to dress her every day! I get so annoyed when people tell me I've wasted my money. I get that babies spit up and have blowouts like 928,374 times a day. I get that babies outgrow their clothes within sixteen minutes, but just let me live. I probably jinxed myself by purchasing so many outfits and she's gonna end up being one of those constantly naked babies. But whatevs, just let me live my best life dressing up my baby in all the OOTDs.

My Rules for Dressing Baby H

Neutrals: I'm talking white, ivory, beige, camel, sand, gray, heathered gray, dusty gray, light brown, wheat, stone, champagne, tan, brown, and black, with pops of muted colors like ash blue, rose, pale yellow, mauve, maroon . . . Occasionally I'll allow articles of clothing in brighter colors, but they best be chic AF.

Monochrome: I just love a monochromatic look, and so does my baby. Monochromatic doesn't have to mean wearing an outfit all in the exact same shade; it also means finding similar shades of the same color. I've never seen a human being not look chic in a monochromatic outfit. It always looks so refined, like you totally have your shit together. And I obvs want my baby to look like she has her shit together.

No sparkles, glitter, or bling: This may come as a surprise, as I can be pretty sparkle obsessed with my wardrobe. I love a bedazzled shoe, and I spent my whole podcast tour in Swarovski-crystal-embellished blazers. But I just feel differently when it comes to babies. To me, sequins on babies equals baby Vegas showgirls. Not that a baby Vegas showgirl is a real thing, and no offense to actual Vegas showgirls, but you get it.

No designer baby clothes: This may also come as a surprise, but I will not be purchasing anything designer for my child. She will outgrow it, she won't remember it, and she definitely wouldn't appreciate it, so it is entirely out of the question. I physically cringe when I see small children in Gucci shoes or Burberry jackets. However, if I'm gifted baby Gucci shoes or Burberry jackets, I absolutely won't be mad and will absolutely make her wear them. I just refuse to pay for it. I have bought many designer-inspired baby clothes. I've purchased so many little black and beige Chanel-looking outfits and shoes for her, so Parisian chic. Designer-inspired, yes. Designer, no.

CHAPTER 12

A Basic Bitch Is Born

My grandfather used to tell me tales of his time as a flight engineer during WWII. The scary moments test-flying planes that had been shot up and then fixed. The hair-raising stories about near crashes and engine failures! That is exactly how I plan to tell my labor story for the rest of my life, just like a WWII vet. The only difference is that there is literally nothing exceptional about my labor story. It's the most average labor story in human history. It went down like a playbook, and I'm not saying Steven Spielberg needs to make a gripping action movie about my birth story, *but it is still fascinating.*

As my pregnancy months trudged on, I became obsessed with trying to induce labor naturally. I was convinced I was going to have my baby early, and I don't know if I was trying to will it to happen by putting out the vibes and manifesting it, but that's how

I felt. Like many women, I didn't realize how bad the last month of pregnancy could be until I was trapped in my giant, painful, swollen body. My pregnancy until that point had gone along pretty smoothly, but the last month was truly the worst. I am so thankful I went past her due date and kept her cooking, but I had it in my head she was going to come on Christmas even if she was due in January. I told Beau many times that Hartford was #blessed because she was conceived on Easter. So I figured since she was a blessed freaking baby, she should be born on Christmas, or at least during the week between Christmas and New Year's, since that whole week is a holiday in my eyes. I thought it would be exciting to have a holiday baby, but Beau was against it. He wanted her to have her own special day on her birthday, and he didn't want her to share a holiday or have people out of town during her birthday for the rest of her life. Basically we were trying to control her birthday, even though we had zero power to do so. Welcome to parenthood!

Now that I think about it, I'm glad Hartford doesn't have a Christmas or New Year's birthday. I want her to be able to say, "It's my freaking birthday, bitches!" just like her mommy used to do. I said that for eight years on *Vanderpump,* so how could I have possibly willed my daughter to share a birthday? My baby has her own day so she can be an asshole on her own birthday just like me. I must have been delusional to think I wanted it any other way.

Before I came to that mature AF realization, I did everything I could to get this baby out. I walked two miles on my treadmill every day. I made Beau have sex with me since I read that could shake things up and get the baby moving. No offense to my husband, but third trimester sex was not pleasant for me. I know some women are like, "I felt so sexual when I was pregnant!" Like, WHAT. THE. FUCK? Who, how, and why? Not only was I so huge I could barely roll over to get out of bed, sex felt like so much effort, and my vagina closed up so much it felt like I was a virgin again. The sex hurt, but I wanted a Christmas baby, dammit!

I also ate spicy food and drank raspberry-leaf tea for a month. I drank castor oil, which literally makes you shit yourself. It's supposed to activate the uterus or something. Didn't work. I put primrose evening oil up my vagina, I ate the salad you're supposed to eat at one of those restaurants in LA that's supposed to be "the labor salad." I ate Taco Bell. Really anything any woman recommended, I did, daily. On December 21, 2020, Saturn and Neptune were aligning, which only happened eight hundred years ago or something, so I wrote about it in my journal and manifested what I wanted to happen on that day since it was supposed to be magical. I spent that entire day manifesting having an early labor. Didn't work. On the full moon of December 29, I manifested again and wrote in my journal and looked up at the sky and prayed, and it didn't work. So I ate more Taco Bell.

I woke up on my due date so depressed and worn out from all the manifesting. I felt like it was never going to happen and that I was doomed to become the first woman whose baby just stayed inside of her forever. Then came the day *after* my due date. Looking back, I wish I would have enjoyed those days of solitude and absolute freedom. Days spent sitting in bed watching *The Great British Bake Off* or rewatching *Bridgerton*. Now I know I am *never* going to get that back. On January 6, I woke up and cried. Beau was like, "I'm so sorry . . ." What else could he say? Then that night, around seven, I was in the bathroom when all of a sudden a little trickle of liquid started coming out of me and onto the ground (here's where my WWII story starts, BTW). I wondered if I had just peed on myself and thought, *Is this where I'm at now? Someone who has lost all control and who is now peeing on herself?* I figured it couldn't be my water breaking because it had a faint pink tint, like a really dry rosé. Beau was like, "It looks like you've been drinking Whispering Angel rosé." Obvs, neither of us are doctors.

I texted our *actual* doctor, and he said that if it kept happening, it was probably my water breaking. I monitored it and kept texting him, "I don't know . . . it's trickling." I was clearly so annoying. He's like, "Listen, you're probably going to the hospital in the morning, so try and relax." I'd had Braxton-Hicks contractions a few nights before, and it was so incredibly painful, so I was nervous, but he made me feel better when he said, "We are in this together." I'm obsessed with my gynecologist. He is so fucking nice. Your doctor is like 50 percent of what makes the birth experience good, so finding a friendly and chill and not-scary doctor makes the experience so much better. Once Hartford was born, Beau and I were actually a little sad we wouldn't be seeing that doctor once a week. I have no clue how he felt about not seeing us, but I'll pretend he was heartbroken.

Back to my childbirth story. I wanted to labor at home as long as I could, not because I wanted to be some warrior woman, but because I did not want to rush to the hospital and then get told we were too early and to go home. EMBARRASSING. I told Beau I was having contractions, and that he should sleep in the bed with me that night. My snoring had gotten so horrible at the end of pregnancy that Beau had to sleep in the guest room. It also didn't help that I got up to pee eighteen times a night. So on that night, I made him suffer through the snores and pee breaks. Most important, I took time to shower and spray-tan myself, fix my gel manicure so there were no chips, and blow-dry my hair so I could look somewhat cute in photos. Make sure to test out waterproof mascaras and primers ahead of time. My number one tip is the spray tan though. You're welcome.

I tried to relax, but it was impossible because my contractions got so much worse. It was incredibly painful, and they were happening closer and closer together, so I did what any self-respecting basic bitch who is about to give birth would do: I went into the bathroom in the middle of the night to do my makeup. The problem was that I kept doubling over in agony, which made curling my lashes nearly impossible—but I did it. I was texting my doctor, but he wasn't responding. At one point I became terrified that I'd have the baby right there in the bathroom while doing my eyebrows!

Eventually we heard from the doctor, who had fallen asleep like a normal human, *but how could he?!* He sweetly apologized for accidentally turning off his ringer, and Beau and I sped to the hospital. We got checked in, I put on the labor "gown," and we got ready to have a freaking baby.

I tried to stay realistic when doctors and nurses asked, "What's your pain level on a scale of one to ten?" So when they asked if I was ready for an epidural and wanted to know my pain level, I thought, if "one" would be like me hitting my funny bone on a table and "ten" was like me burning alive, I should say, "I'm at a four." Beau immediately jumped in saying, "No she's at an eight!" Maybe because I'd been groaning and screaming in pain? Anyway, once he said it, I agreed. I was trying not to be dramatic, but an epidural sounded good at that point, and you know what? It *was* good. It didn't feel great going in, but as soon as it kicked in I was like, *This is the best thing that ever happened to me!* The epidural is what dreams are made of. Totes recommend.

Before birth, I didn't take any classes, which probably makes me sound like a shitty parent. I figured that women have been giving birth since the beginning of time, and I doubt most of them in the Middle Ages took labor classes. It just sounded so boring and so not for me. Even when I read books, I skipped the labor part. I felt like my body would just know what to do, and I figured I would just need the epidural. I didn't even need Beau! I should have just married the epidural. You think I wanted to subject myself to a Zoom labor class? I wasn't thrilled about logging in and thinking people were side-chatting each other like, "There's that girl who got canceled!" No, thank you.

I figured an epidural would be part of my birth experience (I mean, I wanted that shit), but I didn't realize a catheter would be part of the show too. I also didn't know I'd have to get fisted by a nurse to see if I was dilated. I bow down to women who give birth without medication. The doctors and nurses fisted me every few hours, and in between I fell asleep. Beau slept the entire time, because labor is so hard for men. After hours of that, I started pushing the next day at about 6:00 p.m. for about forty-five minutes, and then, twenty-four hours after my water broke, the baby was born! Pushing was actually my favorite part of giving birth, thanks to the epidural. I didn't feel anything except a lot of pressure, like something was going to split me in two, but it didn't hurt. Before the actual day, I thought I'd want *The Greatest Showman* soundtrack playing in the background when I gave birth. Instead, I wanted total quiet, with the lights dimmed so I could stay focused. When I look back, I loved giving birth, because epidurals are the best. Also, because of my daughter.

Meeting my daughter was magical. I will say this though: when she was born and they put her on me, I didn't have an instant bond until maybe two hours later. I was crying tears of joy, but I don't think we should make women feel like they *have* to feel an instant connection with your just-born baby or something is wrong with you. It took me gazing into Hartford's eyes for a few hours to process that this was my baby, and *then* I got attached. At first, Beau and I were like, "She's a demon," because her eyes and hair were black. It took about two hours for me to get past that and become officially obsessed. After we had our skin-to-skin time and she latched on to nurse, Beau made me a margarita. We asked the nurses for permission because we're not maniacs, and that margarita was the best thing that ever happened to me, besides my daughter. And that, my friends, is how my birth story ended. With a cocktail.

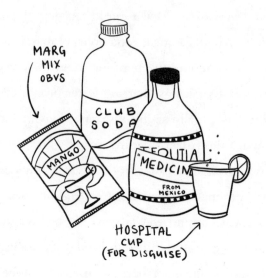

After Hartford was born, Beau was the most exhausted I have ever seen him. He's so helpful as a father now, but in the hospital he was totes useless. Let's just be real. We ate some pizza and Beau fell asleep! I was freaking out, like, how do I know when to feed her or change her?! The nurses left and I was like, *Wait a second . . . I have a baby in here! Aren't you going to tell me what to do?* But they just left us! I stayed up all night staring at her in her little sleeping container thing, and I was so scared. I cried when they took her away to do tests. As terrified as I was, I was ready to go home and be with her and Beau and the dogs and start this new life. Plus, I had a closet full of adorbs clothes and shoes waiting for her. Recovery was way worse than labor because I was swollen, bloody, and wearing a diaper. I felt like a beast, but our baby was healthy!

So in the end, I didn't have a Christmas baby, but I did have a Capricorn baby. I actually had an astrological book made for Hartford called *The Birthday Book*, and it says the time and location of her birth, and it's a whole book about her rising sign and moon. I was so freaking excited about a Capricorn baby. It's my favorite sign because my grandmother was one and she's the coolest person I've ever known, plus Katie is one, and my rising sign is Capricorn. It means Hartford will be responsible, good with money, independent, and resourceful. She'll stick by her truth. I'd love my daughter to be all those things. I like the idea of raising a little independent lady. I'm all about the Capricorn life. The problem is that now when I see my daughter being all independent it hurts my feelings. She's been sleeping in the crib by herself since day one, even though we tried putting her in a bassinet in our room. She was like, *No, thanks, I need my space.* Sometimes I wish she needed me more, but I wanted this independent life for her, so I guess I need to roll with it and be proud of my little Capricorn, even though I *did* have to get fisted by a tiny nurse with large hands in order to give birth to her.

Rock-Bottom TAKEAWAY

Even if a woman gives birth in five minutes with zero complications, that birth story *matters.* My own birth story might not be full of drama (which I am forever grateful for), but it was dramatic as hell to me. I guess, for me, the biggest lessons about childbirth are: No, you cannot really *force* your child to be born on a major holiday. Yes, doing my makeup and hair and some spray-tanning during early labor was worth it. And finally, the epidural is one of the greatest achievements created by and for humans. You don't have to get one, but birthing a basic bitch is a lot easier if you do, at least in my experience.

Pregnancy Bags: Fantasy versus Reality

Fantasy

* Holiday candles

* A mini Christmas tree and twinkle lights so the baby feels joyful AF when she comes out

* My creepy clown

* A plastic surgeon to give me my body back

FESTIVE AF

* Bottomless Aperol spritz pitcher

* My pups

* Bradley, my hairstylist

* A zero-calorie funfetti cake

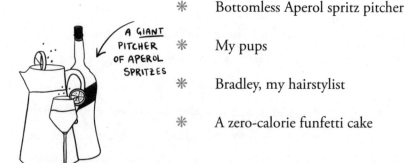

A GIANT PITCHER OF APEROL SPRITZES

* Bespoke silk pj's in the color "Stassi Blue"

* Jimmy Choo bedazzled furry slippers

MY BELOVED CREEPY CLOWN

Reality

* Extra-large slippers because the foot swelling was ungodly

* Black nursing tank and robe because I was sick of wearing a gross hospital gown (plus black is slimming)

* Toiletries to wash all the makeup off and brush my teeth

* Glasses

* Phone charger (obvs)

GLASSES SO I CAN SEE MY CHILD

BASIC TOILETRIES

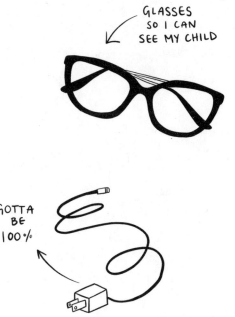

GOTTA BE 100%

· CHAPTER 13 ·

Mom Genes

I was always an independent kid. I blame my Capricorn rising.
That trait has only gotten worse and more intense as I've gotten older. My mom has always understood that I'm someone who
needs space, and she's done her best to give it to me, in between
texts and calls and emails and worrying about me and giving me
advice and worrying some more.

When I became pregnant, I knew I wanted to make an effort
to include my mom in my life more, because I know how important grandmothers are. I loved my own so much, and it was and
is important to me that my daughter has the chance to experience that kind of relationship. Plus, free babysitting! It wasn't until
I actually became a mom that I started to truly soften with my
own mom though, because I now know what it feels like to have a
daughter. I know what it feels like to be my mom!

Are we all destined to become our moms? To act like them and dress like them and say things like, "I'm going to count to three and you're going into time-out!" Or "I'm your mother, that's why!" Obviously everyone has a different relationship with their mom or mom figure in their lives, and mom-daughter relationships can be dramatic AF. Despite what you may have seen on *Vanderpump Rules* though, my relationship with my mom was not and is not always full of drama and tears and yelling. It's just that fights make for more interesting TV than the sweet moments, so when you saw my mom on the show, you may have seen us . . . not at our best.

I always hesitate to use the word *fair* when it comes to reality TV. Reality TV is never *fair*, but that's what you willingly sign up for. With *Vanderpump Rules*, we all knowingly signed up to participate in something that would water down our private lives and sensationalize them for entertainment. The whole point of a television show is to reveal the most entertaining and interesting story. The only "unfair" part as far as my mom was concerned was that I signed up to get paid for this, and my mom did not. She wasn't used to it, so she would get nervous any time she was getting ready to film a scene. It's scary putting yourself on camera! She did it willingly, it's not like I forced her, but she'd usually have a few cocktails to get through it, and like mother like daughter, when we have cocktails, sometimes stupid shit comes out of our mouths.

The hardest scene for me to watch in the history of *Vanderpump* is probably the night in season seven when Katie and Kristen and

I went out with all of our moms. It was my mom's birthday, and I had a cake for her, but we never brought it out because it was such a disaster of a night. Like, Dark Passenger times two thousand—tears, yelling, stress. So not fun. Beau actually had to come over to my apartment later in the night to calm us both down. People have their opinions about me from the show, and they formed opinions about my mom based on a few hours of her life!

The crazy thing is that after her scenes aired, people actually reached out to me about our relationship, or what they thought they saw in our relationship. Actual celebrities I very much admire DM'd me saying that they related so much and they have had a strained relationship with their moms, just like me. I'll never forget when a celebrity whom I'll call Amanda sent me a message and said she struggled with her mom too, and that she had to step back and try to analyze and accept their relationship, which is something I actually had to do at that point in time. It's a very sobering thing to realize your mom or dad isn't the perfect person you thought they were when you were little and that they sometimes make even more mistakes than you do. I didn't talk to my mom for about seven months after we filmed the *Vanderpump* scene from hell. When we finally spoke again, I had to establish boundaries, like the fact that we don't need to talk every six minutes. Now that my daughter is here and I'm a mom too, we've gotten past all that and she's a sweet grandmother. I mean, she handmade Hartford a Harry Potter mobile made of the keys with little wings on them. The base of the mobile is an old-timey witch book that she found on Etsy!

LITERALLY
THE
MOBILE
OF MY
DREAMS

As a little kid, I remember being so attached to my mom at times. I always admired her for being a working mom because the whole concept of mothers who "did it all" and juggled everything really inspired me. Now I have a major soft spot and tons of admiration for stay-at-home moms as well, because both jobs are incredibly hard. Taking care of a kid is *work*. And you don't get paid. Beau and I joke all the time because I have basically turned into my mom, and as much as I admire her, it freaks me the eff out. I thought for sure I'd be a cool mom who gives her daughter space and lets her do her own thing, but I'm obsessed with being around her, and it physically hurts me when I put her in a swing that's just a few feet away from me, like a psycho. At about two months she also started becoming calmer when Beau held her, which hurt! My doula said that was natural, but still.

It does help me understand the times that my mom felt smothering to me, when she was actually just being loving. Becoming a mom has changed me forever. My soul feels complete, and I have a profound purpose in life. I wanted an independent little girl, but it actually offends me that Hartford sleeps better in her room alone than she does next to us. I imagine her saying, *Bitch, this is what you asked for. I'm mature. You asked for an independent lady, and you got one. Now GTFO!* Obviously my baby is way too sweet to say it like that, but I'm pretty freaking sure that's what she's thinking.

One major part of becoming a mom is the whole idea of, style-wise, becoming a MOM. Like, high-waisted, lame jeans, boring sneakers, a short choppy haircut—and not the hipster millennial version of this look. I mean the frumpy, I'm-too-tired-to-care look. When I think "mom looks," I have such an immediate, visceral reaction, as in, *No way will I ever give up on fashion.* Then again, I also thought I was going to be that chic pregnant lady who posted her daily maternity OOTDs and, as I've mentioned, I wore sweat-pants every day for nine months. They *were* cashmere, but still. I also imagined I'd be one of those women who refuses to buy "maternity" clothes, and instead just sizes up at all her favorite stores. Joke is on me, because I *lived* for maternity clothes. Did you see my belly on Instagram?! That thing was huge. Simply sizing up at INTERMIX or Shopbop was not an option.

Since I used to scoff at maternity clothes only to devote my life (for a few months) to them, does that mean I was destined for things like mom jeans and Lululemon pants all day? No offense if that is your thing, it is just not mine. When I was pregnant I would sometimes think, *What if mom jeans are the only things that fit my postpartum body?* That thought made me feel like I was wandering dangerously close to the dark side. I made a promise to myself to remain the chic woman I believed myself to be, prepregnancy and pre-Covid. The one who started a national holiday about getting dressed (National #OOTD Day, y'all).

I may have had ups and downs with my own mom, but when it comes to "mom fashion," she for sure set a high standard. My mom went through a few different phases with her look as I was growing up. It's actually fun to look back at photos and see her fashion evolution, since she was only twenty-one when she had me, so she was still figuring out who she was. When I was born, she was very much into the designer 1980s country club look. She'd sneak off and buy Chanel pieces behind my dad's back, which he would make her return, once he found out. She was always going to the country club with my grandma, and as a young new mom, she wanted to fit in. That meant lots of matchy-matchy clothes, lots of shoulder pads. Think Julia Roberts in *Pretty Woman*. In fact, her character Vivian has always reminded me of the way my mom used to dress and look back then. My mom also had the same curly auburn red hair as Julia Roberts circa 1990. I even think she had the same tan and white-polka-dotted dress as Julia in the polo match scene of that movie, so come to think of it, maybe my mom just watched *Pretty Woman* and took her fashion cues from that.

Several years after the Julia phase, my mom went through her single girl, wannabe–Pamela Anderson phase. My parents had divorced, so my mom dyed her gorgeous auburn hair porn-star blond and started working as a makeup artist. She totally embraced that 1990s supermodel contoured makeup look, and she always overlined her lips. She was still young and now single, so she dressed like a thirst trap in crop tops and skintight dresses. Needless to say, all the boys in my school drooled over my mom, and in high school I started to think the song "Stacy's Mom" was about us. Not a day went by when I didn't hear kids singing "*Stassi's mom has got it goin on. . . .*"

Once she matured out of her MILF phase, my mom started managing a restaurant in New Orleans, and she dressed like Romy and Michele in *Romy and Michele's High School Reunion* when they decided to become businesswomen. She went back to her natural auburn hair color, started wearing chic, formfitting "businessy" clothes, but she still kept her makeup 100 percent 1990s supermodel vibes. As a kid or a teen or even now, I never witnessed mom jeans, soccer-mom cuts, or anything like that. My mom was always the "hot mom," and I guess in some ways that's admirable, even though I had to endure teen boys talking about how hot my mom was. Gross.

It wasn't just about shoulder pads and brow pencil though. Looking back, my mom also set a high standard as far as just being a loving, supportive mom. When I think about my relationship with my own daughter, I kind of just want to repeat what my mom did, so I'm obvs turning into my mother. I would love to be a MILF/hot mom like my own mother, but not in a way that has kids singing songs to Hartford about how bangable her mom is, mortifying her in front of the whole lunchroom. No, thank you. As a kid, I loved sitting around and watching and rewatching romantic comedies with my mom. We'd watch *French Kiss* or *When Harry Met Sally* or *You've Got Mail*. Anything with freaking Meg Ryan or anything super basic but amazing. That was and is our thing. I'm so excited to have that with Hartford, where we can just sit and be girly, even if she's not girly. If she's into *Star Wars*, I mean FML because that doesn't sound fun to me, to sit around and watch *Star Wars* over and over, but I'll do it just to have that special time with her and get in our pj's and quote movie lines. It's called a mother's sacrifice, watching something you hate just to bond and spend some time with your kid. If I have to memorize Yoda lines, so be it.

Another thing that I'd like to carry on from my mom is that she would take me on trips constantly as a little girl and a teenager. She treated me like a companion instead of like an annoying kid, taking me to European cafés for espressos (her) and hot chocolate (me). She'd take me to restaurants and talk to me like I was on her level. We'd hang out. We had fun girl time *all the time*, and I am still all about some fun girl time. My mom would sometimes check me out of school if I had a bad day! She didn't force me to go if I was feeling low and didn't want to play kickball, and we'd have the most fun day together. I still got straight As, and it's not like she would let me skip school every time I didn't want to go to PE (which was pretty much every day). She was not being a bad mom, she was allowing me some days to just take time out. Those are the memories I cherish. She understood me and understood that kids need personal days too. Will I let Hartford skip algebra or gym class every time she complains? No. But I can't wait to once in a while let her play hooky and watch movies with me . . . even if it's *Phantom Menace.*

If you still don't believe that my mom was a cool mom—the

woman took me on date nights! Me. Her freaking annoying little daughter who was into musical theater and the Spice Girls. She would do my makeup, dress me up in her clothes, and take me to dinner and swing dancing in New Orleans at a place called the Red Room. I was nine years old and eating beef carpaccio, which became one of my favorite things ever. I felt like I had the coolest, most glamorous mom. I was so lucky, and can't wait to hopefully be that way with Hartford. I'm going to make mother-daughter time special, as long as she's having fun and feels loved. I can't wait to be her companion and have date nights and girl trips. I want to treat her like she knows what's best for herself sometimes, and that whole experience makes me so excited about mom life. I always wanted to raise a little weirdo who goes by the beat of her own drum, as they say. The whole premise of my last book was about being yourself. We're all unique and one of a kind, we're all born with the ability to beat to our own drum. Your environment and how you're brought up has a lot to do with whether you stay on that path to being yourself, or conform. I have my mom to thank for treating me like an equal, for being as glamorous as she always was, and for inspiring me to share all that with my own daughter. Becoming a mom, I feel like I've been granted access to some exclusive club that no one talks about until you're in it. I've bonded with so many people through DM now over motherhood. I've bonded with my own mom, and Beau's mom, and friends who are moms. Motherhood is basically the new Soho House! And I would not be caught dead wearing mom jeans to Soho House.

Rock-Bottom TAKEAWAY

Despite what you *think* you saw on *Vanderpump Rules,* my mom was and is an amazing role model, and I hope to be half as hot and stylish and understanding as she was when I was growing up. She treated me like an equal and never tried to "change" me or shape me in any way. She let me be the musical-theater-loving, horror-movie-obsessed little weirdo that I was, and I can only hope to do the same for my daughter. She also taught me that you do not have to give up your personal style or your sex appeal or your sense of fun when you become a mom. Just because you're a mom doesn't mean you have to stop dressing with supermodel vibes or going out swing dancing or traveling. What I'm saying is moms *can* be glamorous, with a little effort, a lot of under-eye concealer, and a ton of caffeine.

CHAPTER 14

Having It All

What does the phrase "having it all" even mean?

I seriously need a Xanax just thinking about it.

I'd like to think having it all is just about feeling fulfilled and happy with what you already have, but screw that. Sometimes "having it all" is a big damn lie, especially when it relates to women, and moms, and working women and moms, and all humans, especially when you're at rock bottom, what does "having it all" even mean?

It's freaking hard trying to have it all!

Sure, I want to own my own island where no one can bother me. Actually, I'd prefer to own a ghost town. That way I could appoint myself mayor of the ghost town, and since I really don't know a lot of people who like ghost towns, I definitely would be able to relax on the couch with no one knocking on the door. Do paparazzi stalk ghost towns? Doubt it.

I also want to own a Taco Bell. I want to go to the Met Ball. I would love Hidden Valley Ranch to finally gift me with that sapphire-and-diamond-encrusted Ranch bottle (that's when I'll know I've truly made it). I want it to be Christmas seven months out of the year, and Halloween the other five. A private jet that looks like the Spice Girls' tour bus would be lovely. I'd like Beau to stop leaving his hat, belt, loose change, and keys on the dining room table. I want to be able to naturally fall asleep at night. I'd like to finally see a freaking ghost. A benevolent pet zombie would be nice. If I could have all of these things, maybe I'll feel like I "have it all."

Having it all is actually a lot more basic than a Spice Girls jet. Being on rock bottom can also change your idea of having it all, since you basically have to start from the bottom rung again, and your perspective shifts. Having it all, for me, became less about things and trips (although, I love those things) and more about feeling safe, being in love, having a healthy child, and, yes, fitting back into my size 7.5 shoes. But mostly it became about being fulfilled personally and professionally. And the shoes.

Anyway, it's a scientific fact that there is 100 percent more pressure on women to have it all, and personally I think the way people, meaning all of us, typically think of having it all is a crock of shit. I think everyone has a different version of what it means. I actually loathe that phrase, because there is so much pressure that comes along with it. Women hear it and then get instantly stressed out because we start thinking about things like career, marriage, babies, or a house, or, if you're like me, owning a Taco Bell franchise. What we forget is that sometimes just existing in your robe while feeding your baby is enough. Being on rock bottom completely changed my view of having it all, or being fulfilled. In fact, I thought I *did* "have it all" before it all went to hell. But, after the initial hell, life got so much better.

Facebook COO Sheryl Sandberg wrote in her book *Lean In*, "No one can have it all. That language is the worst thing that's happened to the women's movement. You know, no one even bothers to apply it to men. It's really pressure on women." I totes agree. Back in 1982, old-school *Cosmo* editor Helen Gurley Brown wrote a book called *Having It All*, and it was supposed to inspire women to work and have babies and get married and be successful, all at once! But guess what? HGB (aka Helen) hated the title *Having It All* and she wanted the book to be called *The Mouseburger Plan*. (I mean, what the actual eff?) Imagine if this bestselling book that had advice about pleasing your man and staying skinny and sleeping with your boss had been called *The Mouseburger Plan* instead? Would the phrase "having it all" have become such a big thing? Would there be articles about "being a mouseburger" instead? It obvs doesn't have the same ring to it. So given the origins of this stupid AF phrase, maybe it's time to rework what we mean by it. Even HGB would probably approve.

If you're feeling pressure because you're struggling to balance shit in your life or the masses are rising up to cut off your head, just remember that no one has it all unless your name is Beyoncé or your address actually is the Palace of Versailles. Even then, how would you clean that palace? Would you get lost? Feel lonely? I mean, probably not, but *maybe*.

What if we rename "having it all" to "having just enough" or "having it pretty good"? Or maybe "doing okay today, thanks"! Since my mom has become one of my mom-life role models, I asked her what "having it all" means to her. She said the meaning of that phrase changes as you go through life and have different needs or wants. To her, having it all is about feeling fulfilled, by family or jobs or educating yourself, whatever brings you happiness. My grandmother placed a huge emphasis on happiness, and whenever I'd fight with boyfriends and sulk, she'd say, "You are choosing how you feel about this. You can choose to wallow, or choose happiness." That made it easier to cope. If I had the chance to ask her, she probably would have said, "I do have it all, I have a husband I love and six children, and I travel." She was so peaceful when she passed away. I feel like she left knowing she had it all, and that is #GOALS.

Having it all wasn't even an option for almost everyone on the planet during the pandemic. It was more like how to be happy with the bare minimum, without ever leaving your home. My life became about one goal: waking up happy, or semi happy. We had to find joy in the truly little things, like morning coffee or baking or puzzles or whatever the hell we were/are doing to pass the time. I was happy just stepping outside my door and feeling the freaking sun on my face some days.

I've been working to rebuild my life again and to figure out what I actually need to be happy (Beau, Hartford, some sunshine), instead of what I *thought* I needed (my own Taco Bell). I made a list of things that were nonnegotiable: traveling, friends, work, cute shoes that fit post-pregnancy. I'm just being honest. It's about learning to be happy with the bare minimum, which can include shoes, and learning not to feel like your life is a mess because you don't look like Emily Ratajkowski eleven days after giving birth. For a minute, I felt personally victimized by her mom-bod hotness, but then I calmed down, looked at Hartford, and felt lucky. Not as lucky as Emily, body-wise, but still. I felt pretty good, which is what it's all about, right?

Let's take a moment to examine my queen, Meghan Markle. When she became part of the royal family it *looked* like she had it all, but she wasn't even allowed to wear colored nail polish, and she had thousands of trolls picking apart her every move. And then look what happened—she told Oprah and the world how miserable she'd been when we all thought she had it all, and then some. Then take Taylor Swift. Sure it looks like she has it all, but she can't even go to the grocery store to get some Stouffer's lasagna without someone hassling her. I bet she isn't even allowed to eat Stouffer's lasagna, and that makes me sad. See? Having it all is relative.

Even if you wake up and can't believe your luck, do you sit back and say, "Okay cool, I have it all, so I can just sit back, eat Doritos, and watch Netflix for the next seventy years." If we're going to keep striving, I think we need to rework what that means for each person individually. Find out *your* version of having it all. Maybe you don't want kids. Maybe you don't want to own your own ghost town. Maybe you don't want to own a house and prefer a nomadic life traveling the world. It comes down to your own specific needs and wants, not Meghan Markle's or mine or your mom's.

It's weird to realize that my path to "having it all" started when I became a part of a reality show that was not aspirational whatsoever. *Vanderpump Rules* is such a different type of reality show compared to so many others like the *Kardashians* or *Real Housewives*, meaning that it's not about people who have already found success. In the first season we started off broke, as a real group of friends just struggling and working at a restaurant and dating. I could barely afford food, which is why I was so skinny.

It was the best diet ever. I remember Katie and I had to split $5 foot-longs from Subway. I was living with another girl, and I was late on rent every month. I had so many parking tickets, and I wouldn't have enough money to get my car out of the tow yard so I would have to quickly beg people for shifts at work so I could make money to get my car.

The show started with us hustling and trying to make the dreams we had when we came to Los Angeles come true. No one was watching *Vanderpump Rules* the way they watched the Kardashians. I love watching the Kardashians, mainly because that is not my life, and I totally wish it was. It's a fantasy. They have Christmas parties that are half a million dollars, and a new $400,000 car every month. They get three Hermès bags for Christmas every year. Hermès bags are like $25,000! That's insane. That's not *Vanderpump Rules*.

When the show started, it was the opposite of having it all. We had a server job and our friends. I remember when I came to Los Angeles, I had so many big dreams, like everyone else. I went to Loyola Marymount for college, I majored in English literature because I thought my dream was to write about fashion (because I am basic AF). When we all got the opportunity to be on *Vanderpump*, *The Hills* had just ended and TMZ was all about the fact that *The Hills* cast earned like $50,000 to make an appearance at a club. I remember when my family was like, "How are you going to make a living on a reality show?" and I was like, "Don't worry, I'll make a ton of money just by showing up to a club in a cute outfit!"

The first season they paid us pennies. I mean, I basically paid to be on *Vanderpump Rules*. And when we started doing club appearances it was more like $1,000 instead of $50,000. I quickly realized I was not as fulfilled as I expected to be. I imagined that being on this show would lead to some sense of "having it all," and it didn't. I loved it, but that wasn't the end of the line for me, as far as what I wanted to accomplish. Would I have felt that sense of fulfillment if I had gotten $50,000 to wear a cute dress? Maybe a *little*, but eventually I would have realized that I wanted more. I mean, I don't even like clubs or staying out past eleven at night! I don't know what I was thinking. I'm also cringing thinking that my big dream in 2012 was to do cheesy club appearances. Feel free to judge me. I'm not proud.

The more we talk about having it all, the more I realize how important it is to remember that it's really a state of mind, instead of all the *things* you have. I learned this after seasons one and two of *Vanderpump*, when I finally understood that I had been given a platform where I could actually make my dreams come true. It started to feel possible that I could write a book and design clothes and be creative, and those are things that fulfill me.

Being at rock bottom really forced me to take a cold, hard look at my existence and what it means and what makes me happy. When you're on top of the world, I don't think you think about those things as much. When you're traveling to Europe on JetBlue first class sipping prosecco and living your best life, why would you stop having fun and have deep thoughts about the meaning of life? God, I miss that. But I'm also glad I was forced to reassess things.

One of the main things that kept me fulfilled before rock bottom was being productive and working and doing projects that I loved. It was a hard hit to suddenly not be able to work at all, and my self-esteem was shot. For me, work and self-esteem are tied together, so eventually I had to get resourceful and figure out a game plan. We had a house to pay for and a new baby, and I'd worked too long and hard to build the career I had to just let it go away. I wanted to start over. I realized I missed podcasting and connecting with people, so Beau and I started a podcast about our lives as new parents. It's freeing being my own boss, like a weight is lifted. Obviously it sucked losing all my jobs and everything I'd worked for, but I'm trying to take it all as a chance to be better, learn more, and have, if not everything, then a few things I'm proud of in my life.

I have never written a five-year plan or anything, because I feel like putting a timeline on things can set you up for failure. Like, I didn't get a promotion within eighteen months, so I'm a failure. Screw that! I'd rather take things one step at a time, and focus on one thing at a time. I hate the question, "Where do you see yourself in five years?" Like, aren't I doing enough right now, today? I'm good right now. I want to enjoy things day by day instead of constantly thinking about what's next, because what's next will come eventually.

I guess what I've learned is that surviving rock bottom, pulling yourself out, and taking a hard look at your mistakes and your life so you can try to be better and do better doesn't happen on a timeline. It happens gradually, one step at a time, until you feel pretty good about things. Until you're fulfilled. Why is feeling pretty good not good enough?! I'm not striving for a life that's "perfect" with a Versailles closet that's full of Chanel shoes, although I would not say *no* to that. I'm not trying to be the CEO of fifteen companies or start my own media empire like Oprah (or, maybe I *am* because that sounds legit AF). I would like to become a better, more enlightened (and less puffy) version of myself *for* myself, and for my daughter. I'd like to connect with audiences again and write books (hello!) and podcast and maybe even tour again in sparkly outfits, with Hartford making cameo appearances onstage. Will I one day own a Taco Bell that I can decorate and call my own? We'll see. A girl can dream.

Rock-Bottom TAKEAWAY

Can we all just agree that the phrase "having it all" is bullshit?! Who has it all? People like Oprah have A LOT, but all? And what about moms and working parents? What does it even mean to try to have it all? It's exhausting just thinking about it. What I've learned is that "all" can be simple. "All" can be just enough. There is no set timeline for being fulfilled. It's about what you do, day by day, even on the days you're lazy AF. Find things that bring happiness or fulfillment, whether it's a high-powered job or a freaking soft couch to watch your favorite shows on. It's not about having it all. It's about striving for things that make you happy, and being okay with just enough until that miraculous day when you sit back and stare at your Versailles compound and your private jet and say, "*Now* I have it all." Just kidding. Although a Versailles compound does not sound like a horrible way to live. . . .

CHAPTER 15

Lessons for My Daughter

I always dreamed that I would have a daughter who is confident, comfortable, and proud enough to let her little freak flag fly. Technically we all have the tools to do that, but sometimes it can be a struggle. We're all born unique, so shouldn't we all be living life the way we want to? I feel like so often what makes a kid unique isn't nurtured enough by the people around them. I want my daughter, Hartford, to always feel safe to be herself. One of the greatest things I've ever learned is the power in living authentically. It's what *Next Level Basic* was all about. Embrace what makes you *you*, even if it's considered weird or "basic." It's my job to make my daughter feel safe enough, loved enough, and confident enough to be herself. There is only one Hartford Charlie Rose Clark. Unless there is another one somewhere? If so, please tell me. I'd like to know.

There's so much power in knowing you don't have to conform to anything. That's my biggest lesson: to embrace her uniqueness. It's the most powerful tool she has. She should do whatever makes her happy, unless murdering people makes her happy, in which case, she should *not* do what makes her happy, obvs. I love a good serial killer doc, but not one that involves my daughter.

One lesson that came out of my rock-bottom year is something I never imagined I'd hope to teach my child, and that is to be more thoughtful in what she says and does. Old-school *Vanderpump/* bossy Stassi would be *freaked out* to hear that. I've always just said what's on my mind and excused it by saying, "I'm just speaking my truth and not faking it!" Over time I realized I actually don't like that about myself. People used to praise me for that because I "said what everyone else is thinking," but I don't know if that's a trait to admire. When I see people who think about what they say or do so they don't say or do hurtful things, I admire those people way more than people who "tell it like it is." I hope to teach Hartford to be thoughtful, and to take a second to digest thoughts and feelings. I hope I know how to pass that down. I'm not instinctively like that, so it's a lot of pressure.

It's not just about what a parent can teach their child though. Babies can teach you a freaking lot about yourself, and about life. Hartford taught me about the power of hope, because I was worried about her basically until the moment she came out of my vagina, but I *hoped* she would be okay, especially since we found out she had a hole in her heart when I was pregnant, turned out to be a common thing that should close on its own. Hope is so freaking powerful. It got Beau and me through the days when we felt down. You have to allow it to carry you through tough times. I sound like a cheesy quote on a T-shirt, but it's true. Especially as a parent, because everything becomes scary! Small objects, large objects, car rides, sharp things, solid foods. It's a lot.

My daughter also taught me that—surprise!—life is not all about me. There is a little human who is way more important than I am, and I'm responsible for her. Things could not be less about me right now, and you would think that would bother me but it doesn't. I feel like everything I do now is so she can have a good life and she can make a positive impact on the world, and be happy.

She also taught me that I'm capable AF. How am I so patient? I would never have characterized myself as patient before, but I never get impatient with her. I have to walk into her nursery seven times a night to hand her the pacifier that fell, and I still don't lose my shit. She's given me that. Before you become a mom you worry if you'll be a good mom, and Hartford made me realize I can do this. Of course I have doubts, but I think I'm doing a pretty good job. I think I was totally paired with the appropriate baby. My heart is literally limitless now, which again sounds like a cheesy roadside T-shirt, but I can actually feel that my heart is growing bigger each day. I can't believe how much I love this little freaking baby. I know it's a thing most moms feel, but it's just so goddamn magical. It's like the North Pole on Christmas morning every second of the day. With mimosas.

Is it weird to admit that I feel like I can see into my daughter's soul and see who she is? It all started when she came out of my body just mean mugging. She gives the best side-eye and the best judgy face. Even when this chick is in the best mood, she just seems like a little know-it-all already. She's independent and determined. I feel this quiet confidence with her, like she is secure in who she is already. Do I sound insane? I do feel like she's already in Mensa. I'm making her sound like a hard-ass, but this bitch smiles and laughs all the time too. There is nothing like the vision of her smiling face when I get her out of the crib. It's the best feeling in the world.

The second she was born she was hard-core, already raising her neck and head to look at me, and Beau and I freaked out, asking the nurse, "Is this normal? She's lifting her head!" The nurse probably said, "Oh, she's special," just like she said to all the parents, but let me live in the fact that I think my baby is special. She had gumption! She just popped out of my body and was like, *I want to look and see who this person is that I am attached to.* She gave me major soul-mate vibes. Because she has resting judgy face, she'll probably need Botox when she's like thirteen, but it's fine. She knows who she is. She just got here, and she already knows what's up! How cute is that?

So in honor of my independent, judgy, confident AF baby girl, here are thirty-two lessons I hope to pass along to my daughter, or to you, or to your daughter. Or maybe you hate my lessons and want to create thirty-two of your own. Do it! Make your own list, because motherhood is the hardest, best thing, and there is not one single way to do it. And yes, thirty-two is a weird number, but it's my list, and I was thirty-two when I had Hartford, so thirty-two it is!

Thirty-Two Lessons for My Daughter

* **You will always be loved by me.** As long as I am alive and breathing, you will have someone here on earth who loves you unconditionally. I will always be someone you can turn to. There is literally nothing you could ever do to make me not love you. You could go serial-killing your way around the world, and I would turn you in because I can't have you going on killing more people, but I would visit you in prison every single day.

* **Try to go easy on people.** I wasn't always the best at this. But you never know what someone else is going through behind closed doors. Listen and put yourself in their shoes before you speak.

* **A spray tan is such a confidence booster.**

* **It's okay to take the day off.** "Me days" are important.

* **Always have your nails done.** It's the simplest way to look put together.

* **Never leave the house without at least a little bit of makeup on.** It's the one time you leave the house looking scrubby that you run into that one person you wouldn't want to see you like that. An ex,

your boss, your future husband/wife, Prince Archie Mountbatten-Windsor.

＊ **Listen to your basic mama when I say, take pride in your OOTD.** When you're wearing an outfit that makes you feel good about yourself, your day is that much better. It doesn't matter what it is, just something that makes you feel good.

＊ **When you meet someone, repeat the person's name back to them.** It'll help you remember the name and will make them feel respected. And always look everyone in the eye. I would also suggest you give a firm handshake and let them know who's boss, but this is post-Covid, so who knows if handshakes will still even be a thing. RIP, handshakes.

＊ **I cannot say this enough: You can be whoever you want to be.** So DREAM BIG.

＊ **Make vision boards.** Manifesting really works (but hard work will ultimately get you where you want to be).

＊ **Travel! And not just that, PRIORITIZE traveling.** I promise that I will show you as much of the world as I can, but when my knees give out, you're going to have to take it from there. Never stop traveling. I repeat, never stop traveling. Until your knees give out.

✳ **Have a "year of yes."** Saying yes to things you typically wouldn't do opens you up to new experiences, people, and places. But don't say yes to, like, everything. Like maybe say no to drugs . . . and orgies. Ask your mama one day about her 2016 "year of yes," which for your information did not include orgies.

✳ **An experience is always more valuable than stuff.** I would take a weekend trip with your friends over a pair of new shoes any day.

✳ **Quality over quantity in literally everything.** Food, friends, wine, shoes, clothes, sex. But really take this to heart when you're choosing your friends. Having a few, great ride-or-die best friends you can always count on is way better than trying to be friends with everyone. Also, no one likes a friend collector.

✳ **This is important.** When the time comes for you to choose someone to spend your life with, make sure you laugh with them and that you can completely be yourself with them. Your dad is my best friend and my biggest cheerleader.

✳ **Independence is invaluable.** The years I was single and lived alone were some of my favorite years of my life. Being able to support myself not only gave me the freedom to write the story of my own life, but it also gave me confidence. You've been sleeping in your crib in your nursery since day one, so I have a *maje* feeling you have an independent streak.

✳ **Sometimes you need to be a little selfish.** It's called self-care.

✳ **If you make it a point to be thankful for a few things every day, you have a way better chance of being happy every day.**

✳ **Apologizing is easier than it looks, and it will make both you and the other person feel lighter.** Apologizing (when you mean it) is one of the most powerful ways to nurture relationships. I've been on a few apology tours before, so listen to me.

✳ **Botox is a preventative.**

✳ **Don't mix your alcohols.** I BEG YOU. Pick one thing and stick to it for the night, you will thank me the next day. And always watch your drink.

✳ **Always tell the truth.** There is nothing that will eat you up the way telling a lie will.

✳ **Don't send nudes.** Just learn from my mistakes, please. If you don't want to listen to me, then at least make sure your face isn't in it.

✳ **Always be kind to people in the service industry.** If I ever hear you being rude to a waiter, I'll wash your mouth out with soap or whatever it is moms do to punish their kids nowadays.

✳ **When you get your heart broken, please call me.** I know all about that stuff (my track record is so embarrassing). I'll drive straight to wherever it is you're living and we'll go to Neiman's, drink Kir Royales, and buy shoes.

✳ **Be open to other people's opinions, and don't shut people out because they don't agree with you.** You're a Capricorn, and Capricorns tend to do that, so I'm going to try to get ahead of this right now. Debating is healthy, and fun, if I'm honest.

✳ **Make your bed every day.** It starts the day off right and feels like a mini accomplishment.

✳ **You have the ability to have a positive impact on the world, whether that means you're a great friend to someone or the president of the United States.** You can make the world a better place, even if it's just for one person.

✳ **My grandma Rosemary, who you are named after, always told me that happiness was a choice.** I want you to feel all your emotions, but try not to dwell and wallow in them. When you're down, you can choose to be happy. Why do you think I head to Neiman's when I'm sad?

✳ **This one is important: Always be on time!** Be early if you need to, but being on time is so important to me, it's almost become my defining personality trait. So unless you're in horrible traffic or a plane is delayed, be on time. It's nice.

✳ **Always wash your makeup off before bed.** My mom instilled this in me since before I could even wear makeup: wash your face; take care of your skin. I've never seen my mom go to sleep without cleaning her face, and now I'm obsessive about it. I could be drunk off my ass, throwing up, and I would still manage to wash my face. It's the perfect good habit to end your day with.

✳ **You're going to fail and you're going to fall.** Try not to be afraid of failure. I don't know one successful person who hasn't failed at some point. Your mama has failed many times in small ways and in big, epic ways. Every time I failed, I learned and grew so much stronger. I'm grateful for the times I have failed. They got me here, to you.

Acknowledgments

*O*kay, let's not beat around the bush, these acknowledgments are really about the people who stuck by me when shit hit the fan. It's not easy to ride for someone publicly when you've got a bunch of strangers on social media attacking you for it.

These people didn't excuse my behavior, but they believed that I was a person who made mistakes, and also a person who would commit to bettering myself. The world needs more people like you.

Beau*—Thank you for not only marrying me at a time when it wasn't cool to marry me, but also making me feel like I'm this superwoman who is capable of anything. You are my favorite person, I love you, and I'm lucky as shit.

Lo*—I could not accomplish 80 percent of the things I do without your help, support, and genius brain. I really hope you always know just how valuable you are.

Joe*—You are the one who has been on this freaking psycho roller coaster with me from the absolute beginning. I trust you with my life and maybe even my baby's life.

Natasha*—I will never forget our Zoom call when I asked you to let me start over with an entirely different idea for this book, after I had already written about 70 to 80 percent of the original *NLB* follow-up. I was legit shitting my pants and wondering if you and Gallery Books were just going to cancel me, too. (Just a reminder, I was pregnant, so I couldn't have an Aperol spritz to calm my ass down). When we finished that Zoom call, it was the first true moment I felt hopeful. I will always be grateful for you, that moment, and this opportunity.

Dina*—You could've easily opted out of this journey with me, and I am so thankful you didn't. You always inspire me and you make everything I do a million times better. Thank you for always trusting my vision while always still looking out for me.

Jenna*—It's been a long time coming with this shout-out (lol), but this one is so much more important and special than you could ever imagine. Just that one simple act of kindness when I was newly pregnant (among a million other things) meant everything to me.

Aimee* and Jennifer*—Thank you for keeping this book alive. I know that I owe so much to you both.

Most important, this is really because of my Khaleesis, my supporters. I am so sorry to any of you that felt let down by me. I am so sorry to any of you I hurt. I would never even have had the opportunity to write this if you guys hadn't still stood by me. It feels really self-important and cringy to say, "I would be nowhere without my fans" (I can't say the word *fans* with a straight face). BUT SERIOUSLY, I WOULD BE NOWHERE WITHOUT EACH OF YOU. When I did my first book tour, and then the podcast tour, and I got to meet so many of you . . . I felt so truly overcome with freaking gratitude for all of you. It was like meeting a bunch of best friends who all have the same sense of humor and love of all things basic (aka FUN). I loved watching you guys become friends with each other while waiting in line at a signing, or getting drinks at the bar at a show, or just through the Facebook group. I still will never understand why y'all always show up for me, but you do, and I'm honored and so damn grateful. Thank you for believing that people can learn from their mistakes. That they can make an effort to educate themselves, to look at a different opinion and not see it as wrong but as an opportunity to learn. Thank you for treating me with kindness when I needed it the most. I was literally going to call it quits, move to Italy, and have Beau start an "American hang-over food" food truck. Not joking. You guys have kept me here. Thank you. Thank you. Thank you.

*Not putting y'alls last names for your own protection. LOL.

ㄴ